I would like to dedicate this book to several people. First of all to my late wife Jannise, who was always encouraging me to write a book. To my wife Wendy who in the words of Eric Church, "loves me like Jesus does." Babe, I couldn't do life without you. To two of the greatest kids, Justin and Boo . . . I am so proud to have you call me dad. That includes you to Morg! And finally, to my good friend Keith Allen. One of the most brilliant, creative and well informed men I have had the honor of knowing. Thanks for being a friend and for coming to my rescue.

Table of Contents

Map of the Seven
Churches of Revelation

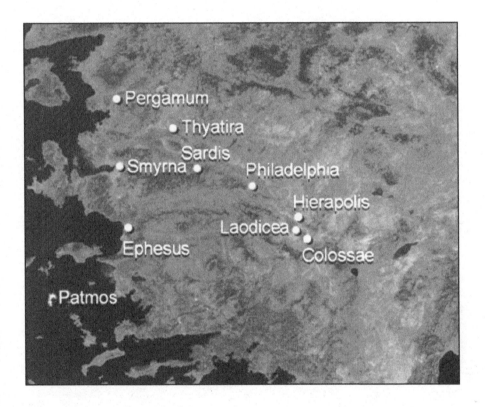

Introduction

H ere it is. The book I've always wanted to write. I never imagined it would take me nine years to finish.

You might be wondering, "Why another book on the church?" Well, there are several reasons why I wrote this book:

First, I have always wanted to write a book.

Secondly, I love early church history. I find the people and culture fascinating.

Thirdly, I find that Christians today are confused about what church actually is. I know it sounds ridiculous for a Christian to be confused about something they are supposed to be, but it's true. That's why I will define "church" in the first chapter.

Furthermore, I'm convicted that the traditional church in America today has become ineffective in this culture. Up until the last 40 years or so the church has had a visible presence in our society. Today, Christianity in America is very on the periphery of our culture.

Now, let me just say that while there are many believers who are sold out for Christ and are doing great things for His kingdom, the impact of the church, as a whole, is sadly lacking. I am not the only one who feels this way. American evangelist, pastor, educator, and author R.A. Torrey wrote: *"We are too busy to pray, and so we are too busy to have power. We have a great deal of activity, but we accomplish little; there are many services, but few conversions."*[1]

English Anglican Bishop J. C. Ryle agreed with Torrey's assessment: *"Surely, no man with his eyes open can fail to see that the Christianity of the New Testament is something far higher and deeper than the Christianity of most professing Christians. The formal, easy-going, do-little thing that most people call religion is evidently not the religion of the Lord Jesus. Oh if you would follow Christ, be not content with the world's Christianity!"*[2]

Fifth, the only way to change the church is to bring true discipleship back into the church. I truly believe most of the issues the church is having today is because of lack of discipleship. I have spent many years looking closely at church websites, talked to church leaders, and I have even had my college students call local churches and conduct surveys. The sad fact is that discipleship in the church is pretty much dead in the water. And it has been for years.

Lastly, I've always been curious as to why there's such a vast difference between the first century church and the modern church today? The late Dr. Howard Hendricks of Dallas Seminary pondered this as well: *"The challenge, the cost, and the conflict . . . those identifying hallmarks of first century Christianity are frequently conspicuous by their absence today. When one reads the pages of the New Testament and relates to what he reads to the contemporary church, he is compelled to conclude that the relationship is more frequently one of contrast, rather than one of comparison. But why? Why the tremendous disparity between the early church and the church today? We are related to the same person. We have available the same power. And we are called precisely to the same purpose. The answer . . . I believe that the early church never became fogged as to their objective. They knew why they were here instead of in heaven. "*[3]

Why is there such a contrast between the early first century church and the modern church today? Let me give you just a few examples on what made the early church different other than the two cultures separated by nearly 2000 years.

ORGANIC

I believe the major difference between the early and modern church is that the early gatherings of believers were "*organic*" and not the program-oriented and hierarchical organizations that we have today. What do I mean by organic?

The following definition is from George Barna and Frank Viola's book, **Pagan Christianity**. "*An organic church is a living breathing, dynamic, mutually participatory, every-member-functioning, Christ centered, communal expression of the body of Christ.*"[4]

The New Testament knows no other kind of church. An organic church is at the opposite end of the traditional church. I like how the late Reverend Richard Halverson described the traditional American church: "*When the Greeks got the Gospel, they turned it into a philosophy; when the Romans got it, they turned it into a government; when the Europeans got it, they turned it into a culture; and when the Americans got it, they turned it into a business.*"[5]

Is the church in America today a business? In many ways I believe it is. Think about it: it's an organization run by professional clergy and elder board or directors, who are usually "spiritually-minded" businessmen. There are mortgages, budgets, salaries, health benefits, taxes and revenue. All of this is to say that the church today is a far cry from organic.

BUILDINGS

Where exactly did the early church meet? We do know that they did not have "church" buildings in which to meet each week. Shortly after the Day of Pentecost, the believers probably met in the outer court or the colonnade area in the temple. Why? Because a large contingent of the early church converts were Jews. If there were Gentile converts, they were allowed into the "outer court" area of the temple. Therefore, it is entirely natural that they would continue to meet in the temple area. The temple was much more than just the place of sacrifice; it was the central point of the Jewish religion and a natural place to go to spread the Gospel to other Jews.

Of course it wasn't long before the Jews rose up in opposition to this new religion and began to persecute the early Christians. My guess is that it was time to find a new place to meet. In the evenings, they would gather in homes for the "breaking of bread." So, for the next 300 years, the followers of Jesus met in homes. During times of persecution, they would meet in places like the catacombs or other out-of-the-way places. Again, there were no such things as "church" buildings. Once their numbers outgrew the home, they would split and start another house church nearby. This continued for about 300 years.

PASTORS

What about the local pastor? The early gatherings of believers did not have pastors, at least not in the sense that we have pastors today. The role of pastor in the early New Testament church didn't exist. The word "pastor" was a metaphor to describe the function of shepherd in the church; it was never originally meant to be an office or title. [6]

TITHING

Guess what? The early believers did not tithe. Yep, I said it and didn't get struck by lightning. As far as we know, Jesus did not teach tithing to His disciples. The tithe belonged to ancient Israel. Tithing did not become widely accepted until around the eighth century, but the early Christians did give. They gave freely and generously from their hearts.

EVANGELISM

Another difference, the early church did not evangelize, at least not in the way we "evangelize" today with our huge crusades and festivals. Actually. there are only three occurrences of the word "evangelist" in the New Testament. (Acts 21:8 Acts 4:11 and 2 Timothy4: 5) Arthur Darby Nock says about the history of the early church: " ... *There was little, if any, direct preaching to the public masses; it was simply too dangerous.*" [7]

The church not only had a message, it *was* the message (Colossians 3:5-6 1 Peter 3:15).

MISSIONS

Not only did the early Church not evangelize, they did not have mission programs. I think the reason for the absence of missions in the early church is the same for the absence of evangelism; the church itself was the mission. Since the church was the mission, they did not send out a separate class of missionaries as we do today. The terms *mission, missions and missionary* are not even biblical, meaning you won't find them anywhere in the Bible. The early believers made disciples wherever they went. They *were* the mission. That was Christ's mandate to us: "*As you are going, make disciples of all the nations, baptizing them in the name of the Father and the Son and the Holy Spirit. Teach these new disciples to obey all the commands I have given you.*" Matthew 28:19-20

COMMUNITY

Acts chapter 2:42 tells us *"All the believers devoted themselves to the apostles' teaching, and to fellowship, and to sharing in meals* (including the Lord's Supper), *and to prayer."*

Unlike today, the early church did not just meet on Sunday's and then rush home to catch the gladiator fights. This verse says that the early believers were "committed" to "these things..." (the apostles teaching, fellowship, sharing meals including the Lord's Supper and prayer). Another way to define fellowship is communities. Imagine what it would be like if five to eight homes would come together in your neighborhood and share all they had in common: food, finances, clothing, medicine. Whoever had need, the other neighbors would pitch in and provide. The first Christians shared their lives with one another. It wasn't about church picnics, potlucks, or small talk in the "fellowship hall." They were real people meeting real needs and joining together to fulfill a real mission. They shared their lives because in Christ they had everything in common. They truly loved each other. They cared deeply about God and His mission on earth, so they joined with the other Christians around them and worked together toward the that goal. Not only did they take care of those within the fellowship, but also they cared for those outside of the community.

PERSECUTION

We need to remember that, at times, the early believers were outcasts and enemies of the Roman government. They were not especially on friendly terms with the Jews either. In its first three centuries, the believing church endured regular (though not constant) persecution at the hands of both Roman and Jewish authorities. People were not freely admitted to the church in the early days. For many years it was underground. You couldn't just drop in to your local church. But when Christians were martyred for their faith in Jesus Christ, it spoke loudly to the world.

Early Church Christian apologist Justin Martyr wrote: *"Though beheaded, and crucified, and thrown tot wild beasts, and chains, and fire, and all kinds of other tortures, we do not give up our confession; but, the more such things happen, the more do others in larger numbers become faithful."*[8]

Here is a true story I would like to share with you. A friend who spent years behind the Iron Curtain told me this story one afternoon.

Back in the early 1970's, when communism still ruled the Soviet Union, a small group of believers met behind closed doors in one of its underground churches. This was a secret church meeting held in the home of the pastor. One Sunday morning the doors burst open, and two soldiers appeared with sub-machine guns. They shouted, "All those who are willing to renounce Jesus Christ, leave now! Everyone who remains will be shot immediately."

As you can imagine, every Christian in that place began to search his or her own heart, and ask, "Am I willing to die for Jesus Christ right now, today?" A few got up and left, ashamed, quiet with their heads hung low. Most of the people stayed.

As the last one left, a soldier shouted, "Is that it?" He held up his gun and repeated, "anyone else?"

Another man rose and ran out. The soldiers then locked the doors, and turned towards the people who remained. The soldiers then laid down their guns and said, "Brothers and sisters, we too are Christians. We do not want to worship the Lord with anyone who is not willing to die for Him! Now that the half-hearted have gone, let's have church!" Maybe we need a little cleansing in our churches today.

THE LORD'S SUPPER

The last difference I want to discuss is the Lord's Supper (Communion). In the early church it was a meal. It was a time of shared celebration, remembrance and joy. How did this celebration of joy become such a somber observance? How did a banquet meal become a thimble full of juice and a dry cracker?

In today's church service, the worship is centered on the music and the preaching. About 10 minutes each week, if that, is devoted to Communion. There is not much time left when you have five or six songs to sing, give a few announcements, pray and then give the pastor 40 or so minutes to speak. Just the opposite was true in the early church. The Lord's Supper, Communion, the Eucharist or the Agape Feast—whatever you choose to call it—was the worship. It was the focus of the early church.

They sang and read scripture, but that was secondary to the celebration of the Lord's Supper. So how did we get our modern version of the Lord's Supper? Well around the mid to late second century, the bread and cup began to be separated from the meal.[9] By the late second century, this separation was complete. Doing a full-blown meal in the church today would cut into the morning church service and cost a small fortune. Thus the cup and wafer replaced the Lord's Supper as it was originally intended. Having experienced a true celebration of the Lord's Supper in real community, for me personally, communion loses something when we partake with a just a dash of juice and a small wafer.

So, as you can see, there are quite a few differences between the early church and the modern church today. You will need to understand the differences as we look at the churches in Asia Minor. These were not tiny Americanized churches. We need to understand them in the culture in which they existed.

In the book of Revelation, we are introduced to seven literal churches in Asia Minor. The disciple John wrote the book of Revelation around 95 AD while he was imprisoned on the island of Patmos. This means that John wrote this book some 65 years after the resurrection and ascension of Jesus, so it has been several decades since Jesus had said, "I will build my Church."

Jesus looks at these seven churches in Asia Minor and says, "Hey, you've had some time now, let's see how you are doing." What we find in these two chapters is Jesus either commending or rebuking each of these churches for their actions. Could these words of Jesus to the seven churches be relevant to us today? Absolutely! Even though we are separated by a few thousand years, we have some things in common.

John writes at the end of each message to the churches: *"Anyone with ears to hear must listen to the Spirit and understand what he is saying to the churches."*

May our ears be open to His Word.

Questions for Thoughtful Discussion

1. If someone asked you "what is church?" how would you answer?

2. Would you agree with the statement that the church today is ineffective? If you disagree, why? Defend your answers.

3. Would the church you attend be considered organic or institutional? Does form overtake function? Is it pro-people or more program-oriented?

4. Before reading this chapter, how much did you know about the New Testament church? Did you learn anything new?

5. What message is your local church putting across to your local community? Do you see true community existing in your local church? Have you ever been a part of a true spiritual community?

6. Why do you attend church? Don't just give the typical "Christianese" answer. Think it through. Why do you attend week after week? Does it really make a

difference in your life? How would you answer those who say that they don't need to attend church?

7. Does it bother you to learn that most of what we call church today is man-made? If you could change the church you attend, what would those changes be?

8. Why do you think the church is so ineffective today? Is there a downward trend in the church? Do you agree or disagree? What can you do to change that trend?

Chapter 1

What Is the Church?

In Oregon, some 30 miles southeast of Portland, is the town of Boring. I love the name of that town. Can you imagine the fun you could have pastoring a church there? I can see myself saying things like: "*Welcome to the Boring Christian Church*" or telling people, "*I pastor the Boring Christian Church.*" You could put an add in the local newspaper announcing, "*Come out and hear the Boring Church choir sing on Christmas Eve.*"

Since this chapter is about the church, let me ask a few questions.

- Just what is the Church?
- How would you define the Church if someone asked?
- What do we really know about the Church, and its history?
- What is its function, its purpose?
- Is there such a thing as "the correct" church?

- What do you really know about the Church?

As I mentioned in the previous chapter, we need to know what the church is in order to really understand Jesus' message to the seven churches in Revelation; we need an understanding of what is the church. We can't just assume that these seven churches are similar to our own modern churches.

When I was a small boy, my mother taught me this little rhyme using my hands. You might remember it from your childhood. It goes something like this: *"Here is the church, and here is the steeple . . . open the doors and see all the people."*

Do you remember acting out that rhyme as a child and wiggling your fingers to represent the people? Of course, it wasn't until I was much older that I figured out that this rhyme isn't good theology. Here is a more theologically correct version: *"Here is a building and on top there's a steeple . . . open the doors because the church **is** the people."*

According to *Webster's New Collegiate Dictionary*, the English word "church" can refer to either *"a meeting of God's people"* or to *"the special building in which they meet."*

The Greek word that is normally translated "church" in the New Testament is *"ekklesia."* The word *ekklesia* appears about 115 times in the New Testament. Surprisingly, in its literal sense, the Greek word never refers to a building or to a place of worship, yet many Christians don't seem to understand that *they* are the church. The church is not the building. Even though (individually and corporately) we are the Body of Christ, we still have a tough time with thinking of ourselves as the church. Let me give you a couple of examples.

As far back as I can remember, our family always attended church every Sunday. Since there wasn't a nursery back in those days, we had to go to "big" church. Whenever we got rowdy, my mother would remind us to behave, because this was God's house and he doesn't allow horseplay. All we ever heard was, "G*et out from under the pew, this is God's house . . . Don't dance on the pew, this is God's house . . . Don't write in the hymnal, this is God's house . . . Don't run in the sanctuary, this is God's house . . . Quit hitting your sister, this is God's house so you better behave."*

Can you relate? That was a common understanding when I was a kid.

Let me give you a personal illustration of how ingrained this message was in me. When I was around the age of 12, I was going through confirmation in the Lutheran church. One evening during class, the pastor asked me to go into the sanctuary to get the candle lighter for him. We were going to learn to become acolytes. In the Lutheran church, acolytes light the candles before the service. I was terrified to go into the dark sanctuary alone. I had no idea how to turn the lights on. It was pitch black except for the small eternal candle they kept lit 24/7 up at the front of the sanctuary. I must have set some kind of speed record getting in and out of the dark sanctuary that night. I was terrified I was going to wake up God or see an angel. It was silly, but I truly believed that God was lurking somewhere in that church building.

Okay, so I was still a little naive at that age, but this thought process continues to this day among many churchgoers. Some people still think there is something special about the church building.

Not long ago, I over heard a young mother in the hallway of a church telling her young kids, "*Stop running, you are in God's house.*" Déjà vu! When I hear people talking like that, I always want to ask them, "*So, where is his bedroom? Does he have a walk-in closet?*"

It is so ingrained as part of our culture. If you seriously think about it, how can you go to something you are? I think you get the picture.

The building is just that—a building, nothing more. There is nothing holy or spiritual about the place. And just for your information, the church furniture and pews were not made in heaven.

So what is the church? Let's start at the beginning. Jesus Christ said in Matthew 16:18, "I will build my church, and the powers of Hell will not conquer it."

The first thought that comes to mind when I read this is, which church did Jesus build? There are some 41,000 different denominations in the United States today.[10] Churches today come in all sizes and denominations and traditions. They come in all flavors from cults to the conservative. Some say their church is the *only* correct church, while others say all churches are correct.

Here is an interesting question. There is nothing really special about that word. I think there was a better choice of words to define church. Why did Jesus use the word *ekklesia* for the word "church?" The answer is, we really don't have a clue. If you went to first century Corinth and asked where the local *ekklesia* was meeting, they would look at you as if you were from another planet. They wouldn't know what you were talking about. Let me explain why.

The word *ekklesia* is derived from two root words in the Greek: *ek* which literally means "out from" or "to" and *kaleo* which means, "to call." So *ekklesia* literally means, "to call out from." As Christians we've been "called out from the world." Which is a true statement. It makes sense, except *ekklesia* is not a religious term. Even though Jesus used the word in the Gospels, there is nothing biblical or spiritual about it. It is a secular term in its usage, and it can be defined two ways:

1. It can refer to an assembly of citizens who were "called out" from the other inhabitants of the city, to consider some matter of importance. [11] In today's vernacular, it would refer to a city council or assembly of councilmen. It is used somewhat as a political term. Oh and I might add that no women were allowed to participate in these meetings. Sorry ladies.

2. It could also be used to describe an assembly of citizens of a particular city or group. The ancient Jewish scholar and historian Josephus gives us a clue to the meaning of *ekklesia*. In his writings, Josephus uses the word *ekklesia* to represent a physical gathering of people— in this case, the Hebrew people:

In Josephus' Antiquities of the Jews 3:84 he writes: "*He called the multitude into an assembly [ekklesia] to hear what God would say to it* (them)."[12]

There are other examples from the writings of Josephus and I won't bore you with them here. As you can see from Josephus' writing, when people physically gathered together, into a physical gathering, they formed an *ekklesia*.

If I "*called out*" a few of my friends to come over to my house for a BBQ and watch football, that could be considered an *ekklesia*. There is nothing really spiritual about that, even if we prayed before eating or called down the "wrath of God" on the opposing team. So if the literal translation of *ekklesia* means basically a gathering of people, how do we come up with the translation of *church*?

When we look at the English word "church," we find that it did not originate from the Greek word *ekklesia*. As far as I can tell, the word "church" comes from the Greek word "*kyriakos*," which is translated "belonging to the Lord."

And again, that makes sense. When believers (people who belong to the Lord) are gathered together, we are, in this sense, a church. Eventually, the place where believers met together became known as "the Lord's house" using the term *kuriakon*. This word made its way into both the German (*kirche*), Anglo Saxon (*circe*), and Middle English (*Chirche*) languages. From these words you can see how we got the English word for "church."

The first recorded use of the word *ekklesia* to referring to a Christian meeting place was around AD 190 by Clement of Alexandria. He was the first to use the phrase "go to church."[13] I don't think his intention was to show that Christians went to a special building, because in those days they met in homes. For the first 300 years of Christianity, Christians did not have special buildings.

New Testament scholar Graydon F. Snyder states: *"There is no literary evidence or archaeological indication that any such home was converted into an extant church building built prior to Constantine.* [14] Furthermore, in Snyder's book on *1st Corinthians*, he writes: *"Until the year 300 we know of no buildings first built as churches."*[15]

The next time we find the word *ekklesia* used is in the Book of Acts. The context for this usage is the Apostle Paul's ministry in Ephesus (Acts 19:23-41). Paul preached the Gospel in Ephesus for two years with great success. Many of the residents of Ephesus put their faith in Jesus and rejected their pagan practices. This caused a huge problem for the trade craftsmen who made a living by selling idols of the Ephesian goddesses Artemis.

23 *"About that time, serious trouble developed in Ephesus concerning the Way* (the original name for believers in Jesus). 24 *It began with Demetrius, a silversmith who had a large business manufacturing silver shrines of the Greek goddess Artemis. He kept many craftsmen busy.* 25 *He called them together, along with others employed in similar trades, and addressed them as follows: 'Gentlemen,*

you know that our wealth comes from this business. 26 But as you have seen and heard, this man Paul has persuaded many people that handmade gods aren't really gods at all. And he's done this not only here in Ephesus but throughout the entire province! 27 Of course, I'm not just talking about the loss of public respect for our business. I'm also concerned that the temple of the great goddess Artemis will lose its influence and that Artemis—this magnificent goddess worshiped throughout the province of Asia and all around the world—will be robbed of her great prestige!' 28 At this their anger boiled, and they began shouting, 'Great is Artemis of the

Ephesians!' 29 Soon the whole city was filled with confusion. Everyone rushed to the amphitheater, dragging along Gaius and Aristarchus, who were Paul's traveling companions from Macedonia. 30 Paul wanted to go in, too, but the believers wouldn't let him. 31 Some of the officials of the province, friends of Paul, also sent a message to him, begging him not to risk his life by entering the amphitheater. 32 Inside, the **people** *(ekklesia) were all shouting, some one thing and some another. Everything was in confusion. In fact, most of them didn't even know why they were there. 33 The Jews in the crowd pushed Alexander forward and told him to explain the situation. He motioned for silence and tried to speak. 34 But when the crowd realized he* *was a Jew, they started shouting again and kept it up for about two hours: 'Great is Artemis of the Ephesians! Great is Artemis of the Ephesians!'"* (Notice the word "people" in verse 32. The Greek word translated as "people" is *ekklesia.* This ekklesia consisted of not just the tradesmen but also the citizens of Ephesus).

35 *"At last the mayor was able to quiet them down enough to speak. 'Citizens of Ephesus,' he said. 'Everyone knows that Ephesus is the official guardian of the temple of the great Artemis, whose image fell down to us from heaven.*

36 *Since this is an undeniable fact, you should stay calm and not do anything rash.* 37 *You have brought these men here, but they have stolen nothing from the temple and have not spoken against our goddess.* 38 *If Demetrius and the craftsmen have a case against them, the courts are in session and the officials can hear the case at once. Let them make formal charges.* 39 *And if there are complaints about other matters, they can be settled in a* **legal assembly** *(ennomo ekklesia).* 40 *I am afraid we are in danger of being charged with rioting by the Roman government, since there is no cause for all this commotion. And if Rome demands an explanation, we won't know what to say.'"* 41 *Then he dismissed* **them/the people** *(ekklesian), and they dispersed.*

From this story in Acts 19, we learn that the word *ekklesia* referred to a gathering of people who had come together for a particular purpose, even though that purpose was to harm Paul and the followers of the Way.

So, let me explain how the word *ekklesia* become a religious term. One of the earliest written uses of *ekklesia* in the New Testament comes from the letters of Paul. 1 Thessalonians was one of the earliest books Paul wrote shortly after he arrived in Corinth around 50 AD. When Paul wrote his first letter to the believers in Thessalonica (an area of northern Greece) he began in this way:

¹ *This letter is from Paul, Silas, and Timothy. We are writing to the church* (*ekklesia*) *in Thessalonica, to you who belong to God the Father and the Lord Jesus Christ.*

The phrase "*ekklesia* in Thessalonica" would have had an established and commonly understood meaning in this city. It could literally mean the "*gathering of citizens who govern the city*" or "*the gathering of everyday citizens of Thessalonica,*" but Paul qualified his use of this phrase and therefore limited misunderstanding by adding

"*in God the Father and the Lord Jesus Christ.*" The Christians gathered in Thessalonica were not equivalent to the civic *ekklesia (city council or assembly).* Rather, they were an alternative assembly. They had assembled "*in God the Father*" and "*in Christ Jesus.*"

The word "*in*" means something like "*by the work of*" or "*under the authority of.*" Paul was referring to the actual gathering of believers in Thessalonica. When the believers gathered together in Thessalonica, they were an *ekklesia.* When they departed and went their way, the *ekklesia* no longer existed. It was temporary. According to our definition, the *ekklesia* in Thessalonica didn't exist unless the Thessalonian believers were actually gathered together. So, when Paul wrote a letter to this *ekklesia,* he didn't mean "*all the Christians in the city wherever they might happen to be.*" Rather, he meant "*all the Christians in the city who were gathered together at a certain time.*"

Let me give you an example. On Sunday morning there is an 11:00 am service at the church my wife and I attend.

Only those of us who are in attendance at that service would be considered the *ekklesia.*

At 12:30, we go to our cars and leave, so there is no longer an *ekklesia.* The building is still there, but the gathering is no longer assembled. Those who are not at the service on that particular Sunday are not considered a part of the *ekklesia.*

When is a church not a church? If we take seriously the New Testament sense of *ekklesia*, then our answer is when the church is not gathered together. To translate a bit more literally, the assembly is not an assembly when it isn't assembled.

One definition of *ekklesia* that I really like comes from Australian missiologist Michael Frost.

He was speaking at the Presbyterian Global Fellowship Conference in Houston, Texas.[16] This is basically my paraphrase of his definition of *ekklesia*. I am not responsible for any of the theological content.

Ekklesia in the ancient times was used in a very particular sense. It referenced a particular meeting that happened in ancient villages. In the ancient days as a village grew it would eventually build a wall to keep its livestock and children safe. There would usually be only one main entrance (a gate) to the village.

When the older men in the village got too old to work, they would turn the business over to their sons. These retired aged men would then hang out at the city gate. They were known as the elders of the city. (For example, Boaz in Ruth 4 and Lot in Genesis 9)

When people had issues, conflicts, problems or questions, they would come to these elders at the city gate. The elders would then discuss these issues amongst themselves and eventually give an answer. The word *ekklesia* is used to describe these elders meeting at the city gate. What do the elders do in a village? What contributions do they make to that society? The answer is: They bring value to the community. It is a better community because of the presence of these men. Just as the elders add value to the village, so should we as Christ's followers.

I love this thought. The church, the *ekklesia*, brings value to the community. As I mentioned in the last chapter, the first century believers not only took care of their own, but they also went above and beyond in taking care of reaching those outside of their community. Just as the elders and those early believers brought value to their communities, the real question is, do we as a church, a gathering of believers, bring value to our communities? My understanding of *ekklesia* is that these followers of Jesus were a gift to the community. Let me ask you a question. If your church was taken away from your neighborhood, would anyone really notice? If they plowed your church building to the ground and built a strip mall, would anyone in the neighborhood miss the church (that is, other than those who were members there)? Does anyone in your community give thanks because you are the *ekklesia* there? Do the people in your community know you? In reality, they probably have no clue what goes on inside your church and honestly, they probably don't even care. We are way too busy inside the church to get involved with those outside of the church.

We don't play with them, drink with them, talk and laugh with them; we don't even invite them over for meals. And then when we try to get them to attend church with us, we wonder why they have all these excuses not to. If you don't spend time with them outside of church, why would they want to visit your church?

We are called to be the salt and light in our communities. We have been redeemed, and we are meant to go into our communities to participate in the work of Jesus Christ in this world. Jesus never meant for us to huddle behind the walls of our church and separate ourselves from this world—just the opposite. What are you doing to further the Kingdom of Jesus Christ?

In one of my earlier ministry ventures, my late wife Jannise and I joined a bowling league. It was a really great way to get to know the people in our community. Once we got to know them, we would ask them over for dinner and a game of cards. It was so easy to do. Nine times out of ten, because my wife and I spent time getting to know these folks, they would eventually show up at church or even attend a home bible study. We never had to beg them to come to church; they would just show up. Do you know what I think?

I think Christians need to quit getting involved in so many ministries in their churches and get out into the community.

Let me strongly suggest that you get involved in your local public or charter school (Sorry, I am not talking about your local Christian School), find ways to volunteer your time in places other than church or a Christian community. Join a bowling league, coach a kid's athletic team, volunteer at your local "soup kitchen." Again, there is nothing wrong with church ministry, but we end up having no time for those people outside the church.

Let me ask you, how many unbelieving friends do you hang with on a weekly basis? Do you even know any unchurched people? The truth is, Jesus never emphasized going to church. He emphasized being the church and going into the world. Jesus never told us to pray that church buildings would be filled. He did tell us: *"The harvest is great, but the workers are few. So pray to the Lord who is in charge of the harvest; ask him to send more workers into his fields."* Luke 10:2

We are to go "into the fields" not into the church. Church isn't about filling a building. It's about filling the neighborhood with the good news of the love of Jesus Christ. Our world doesn't need bigger churches or filled-up small churches. We need transformed lives, families, and cities.

That's hard to do when all the Christians are all huddled inside their local church building.

Again, let me ask you, as a Christian, are you of value to your community? Is your local church of value to the community? You see, before they were called Christians, the followers of Christ were called the "Way." They were called this because of the way they lived. They shared everything they owned; it was a true communal lifestyle.

They shared material blessings with everyone in need out of a common fund. These early Christians brought value into their communities.

In 125 AD, Hadrianus, the emperor of Rome, asked Aristides, a renowned philosopher, to critique the world's religions. After describing various world religions, Aristides responded to Hadrianus with these words: "*But the Christians, O King, while they went about and made search, have found the truth; and as we learned from their writings, they have come nearer to truth and knowledge than the rest of the nations. They love one another. They never fail to help widows; they save orphans from those who would hurt them. If they have something they give freely to the man who has nothing; if they see a stranger, they take him home, and are happy, as though he were a real brother.*" [17]

Look at what the Roman Emperor Julian said some-time around the 4th century: *"These godless Galileans not only feed their own poor, but ours also; welcoming them into their table. Whilst the pagan priests neglect the poor, the hated Galileans devote themselves to works of charity, and by a display of false compassion have established and given effect to their pernicious errors. See their love feasts, and their tables spread for the indigent. Such practice is common among them, and causes a contempt for our gods."* [18]

In the last chapter we talked about the vast difference between the early Christian church and the modern church. If we were honest with ourselves, we don't see local churches making this type of difference in their communities. In Acts 1-4, we find 120 men and women huddled together, hiding behind closed doors in the upper room in Jerusalem. After being filled with the Spirit of God, these few people went into their community proclaiming Christ, and over 3,000 people believed and were baptized. After that, another 5,000 were added. These "hated Galileans" turned the world upside down. Can these things be said about us as the Body of Christ? If not then we need to start now. And it starts with you and with me!

Why? Because we "is" the church!

Questions for Thoughtful Discussion

1. See if you can put an answer to these questions:

    *   Just what is the church?

    *   How would you define the church if someone asked?

    *   What do we really know about the church and its history?

    *   What is the church's function, its purpose?

    *   Is there such a thing as "the correct" church?

2. Here comes the really hard question. Does your church bring value to its community? If so, how? If not, what are some things you can do to begin to reach your community for Christ?

Chapter 2

THE CHURCH AT EPHESUS —
"What the World Needs Now Is Love Sweet Love"

Jackie DeShannon made Burt Bacharach's song "What the World Needs Now" popular back in 1965.[19] You might be familiar with these memorable lines: *"What the world needs now is love, sweet love, it's the only thing that there's just too little of. What the world needs now is love, sweet love, no not just for some but for everyone."*

In 1965, the world definitely needed some love as the United States found itself in the midst of a major conflict with the Vietnam People's Army and the Viet Cong. Thousands of American soldiers were wounded or killed during this conflict. On the home front, there were massive riots in opposition to our involvement in Vietnam. Not only did we have the Vietnam conflict tearing our country apart, but we also had racial unrest to contend with. There were Civil Rights demonstrations all across

the country. The worst of the demonstrations and riots were in the South. Those of us who were around then remember the pictures and news footage of the "Bloody Sunday" riots on March 7th in Montgomery, Alabama. Not a very high point in our nation's history.

In other places across the world there was the Indo-Pakistani War, which caused thousands of casualties on both sides. There was civil unrest in the Dominican Republic and war in Rhodesia (now Zimbabwe). Let's not forget all the sufferings and atrocities that were happening behind the "Iron Curtain."

Unfortunately things have not improved much over the last couple of decades. The US has been involved in conflicts all across the globe, places like Grenada, Panama, Bosnia and Herzegovina, Somalia, Iraq, and the war in Afghanistan. Just recently with the rise of a new Islamic terrorist group ISIS (Islamic State in Iraq and Syria), we may find ourselves drawn into another conflict overseas. There have been conflicts in the African countries such as Libya, the Congo and Guinea. Don't forget that we have been dealing with threats from North Korea for years.

Here in the US, we've dealt with both domestic and foreign terrorist attacks with the 1995 Oklahoma City bombing, the World Trade Center bombings in both 1993 and 2001, and the more recent terrorist bombing at the

2013 Boston Marathon. In just the last few years, school shootings have become more commonplace.

We are still dealing with racial prejudice in this country, and we've added the immigration issues with Mexico to the picture. All of this to say, that we still need a whole lot of love in this messed up world and it seems to be getting worse instead of better.

One of the more popular Christian songs in the 1960's was *"They Will Know We Are Christians by Our Love."* If you grew up in church and are over the age of 45, you've probably sung this song at one time or another. It is right up there with the ever-popular Christian hit, "Kumbaya." If you are not familiar with the song, the first verse goes like this: *"We are one in the Spirit, we are one in the Lord. We are one in the Spirit, we are one in the Lord. And we pray that all unity my one day be restored. And they'll know we are Christians by our love, by our love, Yes they'll know that we are Christians by our love."*[20]

"They will know we are Christians by our love." I am pretty sure that this is not how those outside of the church would characterize Christianity today. In the book **Unchristian** by David Kinnaman and Gabe Lyons, their research shows that half of the un-churched young Americans between the ages of 16 - 29 have a bad impression of evangelical Christianity. They use words like *hypocritical, judgmental* and *insensitive* to describe Christians today.[21] In my own experience I find that I can talk to most people about God and even Jesus without raising anyone's ire. Mention the Church or Christians and it is open season.

So what kind of love am I talking about? My focus is on the kind of love described in the Bible and demonstrated in the life of Jesus. "Love is patient. Love is kind. Love believes all things, hopes all things, and endures all things (1Corinthians 13:4,7)."

Whenever the Scriptures talk about love it is always an activity that you engage in and is never related to feelings. Let me explain what I mean. I can say I love my wife and yet never really show it. It is only by my actions that she can see that I really love her. And so this acting out love to others, showing selfless love, was the quality that set the early church apart from the world. The one thing that Jesus wanted to characterize for his followers was that they loved, just as He loved. That should be first and foremost the message of the church to the world today.

Did you get that? Let me repeat it. *The one thing that Jesus wanted to characterize for his followers was that they loved, just as He loved.* Sadly, I do not believe that to be a true statement in describing the church today.

Remember the story in Luke about the most important commandment?

25 One day an expert in religious law stood up to test Jesus by asking him this question: "Teacher, what should I do to inherit eternal life?" Jesus replied, "What does the law of Moses say? 26 How do you read it?" 27 The man answered, "You must love the Lord your God with all your heart, all your soul, all your strength, and all your mind, and love your neighbor as yourself." 28 "Right!" Jesus told him. "Do this and you will live!" 29 The man wanted to justify his actions, so he asked Jesus, "and who is my neighbor?" Luke 10:25-29

And what is Jesus' response to the man? Jesus goes right into the story of the Good Samaritan. Who are we to love? Everyone! Regardless of their religious beliefs, their lifestyles, their sexual preferences and their political beliefs don't matter. It doesn't matter whether they are rich or poor, black or white, good, bad, or ugly—we are to love them just as Jesus loves them. Boy, if you and I could get that down, it would be a different world.

If you haven't guessed by now, love is the theme of Jesus' first letter to the gathering of believers in Ephesus. Ephesus was a fascinating city. The ancient city was located on the left bank, near the mouth of the Cayster River. The great thing about the Cayster River is that it was deep enough so you could bring large ships upstream into the artificial harbor of Ephesus. The downside of the Cayster River was that it also brought silt upstream that would fill up the harbor, making it unusable.

After dredging the silt deposits from the harbor for centuries, the Ephesians decided that it would be simpler to just move their city to a new area accessible to the river. Ephesus was in fact moved four times during its history before being abandoned in the 13th century. The last harbor actually sits some six miles from the river. [22]

The silt filling the harbor would eventually make it too difficult for larger ships to get into Ephesus.

That could be why Paul chose to meet the elders of Ephesus at Miletus, some miles away when he visited them later in Acts 20:17

Politically, Ephesus was the capital of the province. It was considered one of the "free cities" by Rome. That meant that the city had special privileges that other cities did not. Even though there was a Roman governor who resided there, the city was self-governed, meaning they were allowed to coin their own money and operate their own city council without interference by Rome.

Economically, Ephesus was a powerhouse. Not only was it a busy seaport; it also had three major roads from various continents running through the city. There was a constant flow of traffic from all over the world.

One of the first sights seen by those sailing into the harbor of Ephesus would be the Temple of Artemis—one of the Seven Wonders of the Ancient World. It took some 220 years to build. It measured 361 feet long and 180 feet wide. It had 127 columns, which stood 60 feet tall. These columns were inlaid with gold.[23] Can you imagine sailing into the harbor and seeing this magnificent temple with the sun glittering off those golden columns?

One ancient writer testified: *"I have seen the walls of the hanging gardens of Babylon, the statue of Zeus of Olympia, the Colossus of Rhodes, the lofty pyramids, the Pharos of Alexandria and the ancient tomb of Mausolus. But when I beheld the temple at Ephesus towering in the clouds, all these other marvels were eclipsed."* [24]

The goddess Artemis was one of the most widely respected and highly worshipped deities of the ancient Greeks. Her Roman equivalent would be the goddess Diana. The original temple was built sometime around 550 BC and destroyed by fire in 356 BC. A man named Herostratus, set fire to this temple in order that his name would be remembered. He had no issues with the worship of the goddess; he just wanted to be famous. It worked. The temple was re-built twice, on a more modest scale. The Goths later destroyed the first building while the second was completely laid to waste by a Christian mob led by the archbishop of Ephesus, John Chrysostom in 401 AD.

To the Ephesians, Artemis was the goddess of fertility. If you have ever seen pictures depicted of this goddess, they can be somewhat disturbing.

Around the base of the Ephesian idol, there were carved mystic inscriptions and cryptic messages. Priests would copy these inscriptions on parchment and then sell them as charms to ward off disease, demons, and bad luck.[25] These parchments were called "Ephesian Letters." Many of those travelling to Ephesus would purchase one of these "Ephesian letters" to insure that they were going to be healthy and lucky.

There were artisans and craftsmen who sold their wares from booths around the temple. These artisans made replicas of the popular idols out of silver and other metals for worshippers to purchase and take home with them. These worshippers would then take these idols to make worship centers in their homes or places of business.

We saw in the last chapter that when people began to turn to Christ under the ministry of the apostle Paul, the idol makers, led by a silversmith named Demetrius, held a meeting which erupted into a riot with thousands chanting "Great is Artemis of Ephesus." (Acts 19: 23-41)

So what went on in the temple on a daily basis? Normally what most people are familiar with were the male and female prostitutes who would sell their "wares" as worship to Artemis. And yes, sex was a big part of the worship of Artemis. Every devotee to Artemis whether male or female served two years in the temple with most of their earnings going into the temple treasury. What was the temple treasury? It served basically as a bank. Let's say you were a merchant who travelled into Ephesus to sell your goods. The temple treasury would act as a bank for you. It not only served the local merchants, but for merchants all over the Roman Empire. Not only was the temple a place to keep your money, it was also a museum in which the best statuary and most beautiful paintings were preserved.

The grounds of the temple of Artemis served as sanctuary for the those seeking refuge from the law. If you were wanted for any crime and you could get within the grounds of the temple, you could not be arrested. Something like a kid's game of tag. If you could get to base before you were caught, you would be safe. So naturally, just outside the temple, there were small hamlets in which thieves, murderers and other sordid characters made their homes. It had become so out of control over the years that eventually the emperor Tiberius changed the law.

The Ephesian philosopher Heraclitus once said of the people of Ephesus: *"the animals and the inhabitants of Ephesus were fit to be drowned."* [26]

Probably not a great place to raise a family. Ephesus offered other attractions besides the temple. It had all the amenities of a modern city. The main street through Ephesus was called the Arcadian. This street was 100 feet wide, paved with marble slabs and mosaics. Both sides of the street were filled with shops and galleries.

At night, lanterns would be lit for all the activities on the streets. That was a luxury many cities could not afford. There were beautiful fountains, such as the Fountain of Trajan. The Water Palace at Ephesus was probably the largest building in the city. It acted as a reservoir to supply water to the entire city. They even had public baths where the rich could gather for socializing. There were separate sections for cold water, warm water and hot water. How did they provide the hot water? The water was piped underground and heated in furnaces. They even had public toilets so large that they could accommodate 50 people at one time. These public facilities were situated over a canal of running water that flowed into the city sewer system, which ran the sewage underneath the main streets.

The theater at Ephesus was built into the side of Mt. Pion and could hold 25,000 spectators. The great uproar that Paul caused in Acts 19 took place in this stadium.

Ephesus was also known as a center of learning. Ephesus had a large, two-story library called the Library of Celsus. Thousands of parchment and papyri were stored there. It was the third richest library in the ancient world. Ephesus was also the birthplace of the Pre-Socratic philosopher Heraclitus and boasted of having a school of philosophy.

Women also enjoyed equal rights and privileges with men. There were women artists, painters and teachers. [27]

As you can tell, Ephesus had it all. They had gymnasiums as well as arenas where gladiators would entertain the crowds by fighting wild animals or each other to the death. In writing to the Corinthians, Paul mentions the fighting of wild beasts. (1 Corinthians 15:32)

The wealth and luxury of the city gave them an independent *"we don't need anyone attitude."* The Ephesian's were well known for their arrogance. If you were Ephesian you felt as though you were *"something special."*

For example, when Alexander the Great came to Ephesus in 333 BC, the temple was still under construction. He offered to finance the completion of the temple if the city would credit him as the builder. The city fathers didn't want Alexander's name carved on the temple, but didn't want to tell him that. They finally gave the tactful response: *"It is not fitting that one god should build a temple for another god."* Alexander didn't press the matter. [28]

Within this wealthy, immoral, pagan and arrogant culture, God decided to place a church.

Paul planted the church in Ephesus during his second journey and eventually the disciple John became its shepherd. Lets look at Jesus' message to those believers in Ephesus. Revelation 2:1: *"Write this letter to the angel of the church in Ephesus. This is the message from the one who holds the seven stars in his right hand, the one who walks among the seven gold lampstands:"*

You will notice that Jesus speaks of seven stars and seven gold lampstands. This description by John is easy for the church in Ephesus to understand. John defines stars and lampstands in chapter 1:20: *"This is the meaning of the mystery of the seven stars you saw in my right hand and the seven gold lampstands: The seven stars are the angels of the seven churches, and the seven lampstands are the seven churches."*

So there is no guessing as to what these descriptions mean. Pretty straight forward. The word angel is the word *"angelos"* which simply means messenger. When we hear the word angel that is usually the picture that comes to mind. But if you think about it, that's what an angel does in Scripture. Angels were messengers of God. In this case the angel of the church would be the one taking John's message to the church. Some believe this is to be the pastor of the church of Ephesus, since pastors give messages. But that is not necessarily true. As I mentioned in an earlier chapter, the pastor was not an office or title as we find in the modern church today. Pastor was a metaphor to describe a particular function in the church.

The Greek word for pastor is *"poimenas."* It simply means shepherds (plural). (Ephesians 4:11)

A first century shepherd had nothing to do with the specialized and professional position that it has come to have today in contemporary Christianity.

The angel in the church of Ephesus could have been anyone in leadership. Jesus addressed this letter to the messenger of this church to be read when they gathered as a body on the Lord's Day.

So in the first verse of the second chapter of Revelation, we see Jesus holding the "seven stars" (messengers) in his right hand and walking amongst the "seven golden lampstands" (the churches).

Do you know what I love about this verse? I love the idea that Jesus is walking amongst us.

When we gather together as the church, He is there with us. When we gather just as the believers in Ephesus did, He is there with us, watching over us.

Look at the next two verses. Revelation 2:2-3: "*I know all the things you do. I have seen your hard work and your patient endurance. I know you don't tolerate evil people. You have examined the claims of those who say they are apostles but are not. You have discovered they are liars. You have patiently suffered for me without quitting.*"

Do you see those seven words, "*I know all the things you do?*" On one hand, it is reassuring to know that Jesus is watching over us. The other side of the coin is that He knows all the things we do and hears every thought. In each message to the seven churches, Jesus states, "I know." Often, we go through our daily life and forget that there is a God who is watching our every action. He knows all of our thoughts and sees our true motives. Remember that the next time you decide to blatantly walk into sin; He sees all. Nothing we do is hidden. There are no secrets, even the acts we do in private.

In Psalm 139, David puts it this way: *"Oh Lord, you have examined my heart and you know everything about me. You know when I sit down or stand up. You know my thoughts even when I am far away.*

You see me when I travel and when I rest at home. You know everything I do. You know what I am going to say even before I say it, LORD."

The fact that He "knows all things" should temper our actions because one day we will be judged accordingly (1 Corinthians 3:12-15; 2 Corinthians 5:9-10).

So as Jesus observes these believers in Ephesus, He applauds them. He says of them, *"I have seen your hard work and your patient endurance."* Notice the *"patient endurance."* What was going on with the Ephesian believers that Jesus would need to encourage them to be patient and endure? We do know that there was scattered persecution from the Roman emperors towards the Christians in Asia minor. We also know that the Jews were persecuting Christians. In his Apologeticum (The Apology), Tertullian chuckles at how the Christians were always in the wrong, no matter what happened: *"If the Tiber rises too high for the walls, or the Nile too low for the fields, if the heavens do not open, or the earth does, if there is famine, if there is plague, instantly the howl is, 'The Christians to the lion!' What, all of them, to a single lion?"*[29]

Tertullian's point was that people persecuted and hated Christianity irrationally, and then looked for reasons to justify that persecution. Remember that Ephesus was a pagan city devoted to the goddess Artemis. It was filled with debauchery and immorality. The believers in Ephesus were definitely being persecuted. The Apostle Paul wrote both books, first and second Corinthians, from Ephesus. Notice Paul's words to those believers in Corinth:

" . . . If from human motives I fought with wild beasts at Ephesus, what does it profit me?" 1 Corinthians 15:32 NIV

Could Paul have been fighting beasts in the arena? We really don't know. Paul writes later, " . . . We do not want you to be uninformed, brothers, about the hardships we suffered in the province of Asia. We were under great pressure, far beyond our ability to endure, so that we despaired even of life. Indeed, we felt we had received the sentence of death . . . He has delivered us from such a deadly peril, and he will deliver us again." 2 Corinthians 1:8-10.

So there is evidence that life in Ephesus was difficult for the believer. Jesus is telling them to continue working hard to further the kingdom of God and to endure these hardship patiently.

How many times do we endure hardship patiently? Honestly, I am not a patient person. I'm more of a whiner, just ask my wife.

How well do you endure the tough things of life? Being patient is something that our culture is amazingly poor at. If our internet takes more than a couple seconds to load a page, we get impatient. Smart phone apps eliminate the need to ask for directions, or reserve a table at a restaurant. We can have movies and TV shows streaming in our homes in seconds. And yet "waiting" seems to be a major theme in scripture.

Here are just a couple of examples: Abraham and Sarah waited decades for the promise of a son to be realized; Joseph waited three years in prison for a crime he didn't commit. Have you ever heard the term "the patience of Job?" How about Simeon and Anna waiting for the announcement of the Messiah? Those of you old enough . . . remember having to wait three years for the next Star Wars movie to come to the theaters?

Here in this passage we find Jesus commending the believers in Ephesus for their patient endurance. This whole passage is written within the backdrop of adversity. Life was not easy for the Ephesian believers. Jesus was saying, "I understand what you are going through."

Look at what James has to say about patiently enduring trials. 2 *"Dear brothers and sisters, when troubles come your way, consider it an opportunity for great joy. 3 For you know that when your faith is tested, your endurance has a chance to grow. 4 So let it grow, for when your endurance is fully developed, you will be perfect and complete, needing nothing."* James 1:2-4

So Jesus commends them for their hard work and patient endurance. Then He lauds them for their discernment and their intolerance of evil people. They examined those who called themselves apostles and found them out to be liars. The church at Ephesus refused to compromise their moral or doctrinal purity. 1 John 4:1 tells us: *"Dear friends, do not believe everyone who claims to speak by the Spirit. You must test them to see if the spirit they have comes from God, for there are many false prophets in the world."*

The church had "put to the test" these visiting apostles and teachers. They found their doctrinal claims to be in error. When Paul was on his way to Jerusalem, he stopped in Miletus and met the Elders from Ephesus. He told them, "29 *I know that false teachers, like vicious wolves, will come in among you after I leave, not sparing the flock. 30 Even some men from your own group will rise up and distort the truth in order to draw a following. 31*

Watch out! Remember the three years I was with you—my constant watch and care over you night and day, and my many tears for you."

I think a few words are needed here. This discernment and intolerance for false teachers and apostles is really needed in the church today. What really sets me off are the numbers of "Christians" who so willingly follow false teachers. It is so obvious by the words coming out of their mouths or the pages of their books that they are teaching false doctrine. Yet, "Christians" continue to fill stadiums for their conferences and buy their books and materials.

John warns us to beware. As followers of Jesus we need to call out these men and women and warn others of their false teachings and writings. Honestly, I know it is easier said than done. I have learned how difficult it is from first hand experience. Timothy warns us of false teachers in 2 Timothy 4:3, *"For a time is coming when people will no longer listen to sound and wholesome teaching. They will follow their own desires and will look for teachers who will tell them whatever their itching ears want to hear."*

Is this happening today? Are Christians out there looking for teachers who will "tickle their itching ears?" Sadly, more than ever before. Let's just take the evangelist and healer Benny Hinn as an example. Benny has been accused as a false prophet over the years for his doctrinal error; giving false prophecies and false healing claims. He has been accused of financial impropriety as well as living a lavish lifestyle. Can we attach the "false prophet" tag on Benny? I believe Benny falls into the "false prophet" category. Here are just a few of his so-called prophecies and nonsensical statements:

On Dec. 31, 1989, Hinn went into a trance and said God was giving him (in real time) prophecies about major events that would occur before the end of the next decade. What events?

- *The total collapse of the American economy.*
- *Sometime during the 1990s earthquakes would ravage the East Coast*
- *A female would be elected as president.*
- *Fidel Castro would die in office.*
- *The rapture of the church would occur.*
- *The homosexual community of America would be destroyed by fire "in '94 or '95, no later than that."*[30]

Is Benny a prophet of God? According to what the scripture says about requirements to be a prophets of God, Benny is nowhere close. And yet today he still sells tons of books and has thousands of followers who attend his crusades and hang on his every word. He is just one of many wolves out there who are preying on those who *"will reject truth and chase myths."* 2 Timothy 4:4

Jesus commends the believers in Ephesus for their discernment and intolerance of these evil people. About 15 years after John had written Revelation, Ignatius wrote to the believers of Ephesus and commended them for refusing to give a home to any heresy. [31]

Could Jesus applaud you and your church for its discernment and intolerance of evil? How is your discernment? Do you follow anyone who is considered a "false prophet" or "teacher" today?

I want you to notice that the first four churches in this list of seven dealt with false teachers (Revelation 2:2, 6, 9, 14-15, 20).

Now the "warm fuzzies" end and Jesus turns up the heat. Look at verse 4 and 5. 4*"But I have this complaint against you. You don't love each other or me as you did at first!* 5 *Look how far you have fallen! Turn back to me and do the works you did at first. If you don't repent, I will come and remove your lampstand from its place among the churches."*

Notice Jesus says to the Ephesian believers, *"You don't love me or each other as you did at first!"*

Jesus literally saying, "You have abandoned . . . you have lost the love you had for me at first."

First love is an interesting phrase. In the Greek they didn't have the punctuation that we have today. Today we have *italics* . . . we have **bold face** . . . we can <u>underline</u> . . . we can change the color and emphasize with exclamation points!!!

In the early Koine Greek they didn't have any of that. So to emphasize a word they would put it out of order. So that when you are reading it you think, "Huh! Oh, so that is what's being said?"

This statement does not suggest that they no longer had any love for Christ. Rather, it means that the quality of their love for Him had weakened. The Greek word translated "you have abandoned" means just that . . . "to abandon, depart, forsake, and neglect."

I have this ongoing problem. I am always losing things. I lose my cars keys, cell phone, wallet. I have actually lost my car at the airport more times than I care to admit. My mother used to say that "if my head wasn't attached I would lose it." When you lose your car keys, where are they? When you lose your cell phone, where is it? If you think real hard about it, when you lose your car keys or your cell phone, they're right where you left them! And that's the way it is with your first love for Jesus. If you've lost it, guess where it is. It's wherever you left it. Jesus says, go back and find it. Wherever it is, He is still there because He hasn't moved! He's waiting for you to come back.

It's kind of like the old joke about the road-line painter. You know the guys who used to paint the lines on the road before the machines took over. This guy got a job working as a line painter. The first day he set a record by painting four miles. It was a new company record. The second day he painted two miles, which was still above average. The third day he painted only one mile. On the fourth day he painted only 200 yards. So the boss brought him into the office to ask what was going on? The guy said, "Well I just kept getting further and further away from the paint bucket." I know, it's kind of a dumb but the point is this. Jesus hasn't moved—we have—and we need to return to Him.

Remember the phrase from a song made popular by the Righteous Brother's . . . *"Baby, you've lost that loving feeling?"*[32] Have you lost your "loving feeling for Jesus? Where is Jesus on the list of your priorities?

Let me ask you a question. Do you remember the first time you fell in love with Jesus? Have you ever in your life loved the Lord so much that He was on your mind constantly and all you wanted to talk about your relationship with him? Is it still that way today or have you "lost that loving feeling for him?"

Is this a serious problem? Absolutely! Remember what Jesus said that the greatest commandment was? *"You must love the LORD your God with all your heart, all your soul, and all your mind. This is the first and greatest commandment."* Matthew 22:37,38

How do you do that? How do you love the Lord your God with everything you have? I have read this verse thousands of times and even put it to memory. But I found that reading it over and over again and memorizing the verse didn't make it happen in my life, no matter how much I wanted it to. As Christians we like to think that Jesus has first place when in our lives when in reality he is probably nowhere close. How do you begin to love the Lord your God with all your heart, soul and mind? You start with obedience to His Word. To put it in simple terms, whatever he says you do it! Simple obedience.

Jesus made it pretty clear what your life should look like if you really love Him. If you truly love Him you will be obedient. John 14:15 says this: *"If you love me, obey my commandments."*

Jump down to verse 21: *"Those who accept my commandments and obey them are the ones who love me. And because they love me, my Father will love them. And I will love them and reveal myself to each of them."*

So let me ask you, how are you doing in the area of obedience? It is one thing to say you love Him, but it is completely another thing to actually obey Him. If you want to regain that "first love" feeling for Jesus, start being obedient. And that road begins with repentance.

Look at verses 5: "*Look how far you have fallen! Turn back to me and do the works you did at first. If you don't repent, I will come and remove your lampstand from its place among the churches.*"

Notice three things from this verse. First of all Jesus says, "*look how far you have fallen.*" Some versions translate it "remember" how far you have fallen. The Greek word translated "fallen" means that they were in a state of spiritual decline. This was more than an occasional slip.

Secondly, because they had fallen away they needed to repent. The English word "repent" conveys the idea of sorrow or contrition.

Today's definition would be more along the lines of "crud, I got caught." That is not repentance.

The Greek word does not carry that idea; it is more of a total change of thought and behavior. It basically means to change ones mind and turn around and walk the other way. It is clearly connected with changed behavior, as seen in the following phrase "*and do the deeds you did at first.*"

Third, we need to do those things we did at first that made us close to the Lord. Which is what? Repent and obey.

I like the advice James that gives in his epistle, 8"*Come close to God, and God will come close to you. Wash your hands, you sinners; purify your hearts, for your loyalty is divided between God and the world. 9 Let there be tears for what you have done. Let there be sorrow and deep grief. Let there be sadness instead of laughter, and gloom instead of joy. 10 Humble yourselves before the Lord, and he will lift you up in honor.*" James 4:8-10

That sounds like repentance to me. The believers in Ephesus did not notice how far they had fallen and were unrepentant, so Jesus warns them: "*I will come and remove your lampstand from its place among the churches.*"

Jesus is not afraid to give an "or else" to the believers in Ephesus. He states that He will come in judgment to discipline His church for having a cold heart towards Him. Jesus always disciplines those He loves (Hebrews 12:6; 1 Pet 4:17). He would not love His church if He did not discipline it. If you are a parent with kids, you will understand this last sentence. In this case this is a collective discipline of the entire church. Jesus says that He will remove the church in Ephesus from a sphere of effectiveness or possibly out of existence totally. The removal of the lampstand is clearly figurative language. Does it refer to eternal damnation? No, of course not! Nothing in the context supports this. Rather, what is in view is temporal in nature. If the church did not repent the Lord would remove the church's ability to bear witness for Him. When this occurs, the light of the church goes out and results in the church no longer having an impact on its neighborhood or its world. So what about the church in America today? Could our lack of being salt and light in our nation today be the result of God's discipline of removing our lampstand? I don't think so . . . at least not yet. But the clock is ticking! But I do believe that the Church in the United States is in a very similar situation to the believers in Ephesus.

We have definitely lost Jesus as our first love. In my opinion, the "church" itself has become an idol in America. We have these "rock-star pastors" who we worship. We tend to focus on the dream of having these huge successful ministries. We compete with the other churches down the street trying keep the people in "our" churches. Just the other day I heard a local pastor say that he had to get rid of several staff because they didn't fit into the program for his church.

Yes, you heard him right, "his church."

Oh, that is so very wrong. Everything today seems to be all about the church and its programs. Jesus says we need to repent and look to see how far we have fallen. It is a sad statement about the church when all the statistics tell us that there is little if any difference between those who call themselves Christian and those who don't. We think that we can continue living in our sin and still have a good relationship with Jesus. Where is the repentance? Where is the obedience? The Church in America needs to repent and become obedient or else God will pull the plug on our lampstand.

I have heard people say, "well surely God will not let His church in America die?" I wouldn't be too sure about that. Let me ask you, historically, what happened to the church in Ethiopia? Up until about 330 AD, Ethiopia was a strong bastion of Christianity. Where is this stronghold of the faith now?

How about the church that was in Damascus? History teaches us that we cannot assume divine intervention. Christianity in the west could easily weaken and disappear.

Honestly, in my opinion, I truly believe we are well on our way. This eventually happened to the church in Ephesus when Islam invaded Turkey and wiped out Christianity. As far as we know there is no church in Ephesus today, or much of one in the modern city of Kushadesi, nearby. The country of Turkey, where all seven of these churches were located, is more than 98 percent Muslim today, a Mecca of false religion and a vast spiritual desert. Could there be believers in this area today? I am sure there are, but they are probably small in number and possibly underground.

What is true in Turkey is also true elsewhere. Did you know that in the United States 4,000 new churches begin each year and 7,000 churches close their doors. [33] This is serious stuff—no love, no light! The church that loses its love will soon lose its light, no matter how doctrinally sound it may be. When love and unity is missing, ministry stops and religious activities take its place.

Preachers continue to preach, congregations continue to congregate, programs continue to run, but there isn't a flicker of life—or light—because the love is gone.

Jesus finishes off His letter to the Ephesians with another commendation. Look at verse 6: *"But this is in your favor: You hate the evil deeds of the Nicolaitans, just as I do."* Though they had left their first love they had not left their former hatred for evil. Note how sensitive Jesus' heart is toward His church. He guards against deflating them by concluding with a note of praise. *"You hate the evil deeds of the Nicolaitans, just as I do."*

There is much confusion today as to who these Nicolaitans were. They appear again in the letter to the church at Pergamum, and we will discuss them in greater detail there.

Notice that Jesus didn't say he hated the Nicolaitans, but that he hated their deeds. There is a big difference between hating the things someone does and hating the individual. Remember, love is what this whole letter is about.

Some of you may be saying at this point, "So you are saying to love the sinner and hate the sin?"

No I am not. In actuality, I personally dislike that phrase. Why? One, because it's not in the Bible. Secondly, I believe that it is just a catch phrase that Christians like to use and don't really mean it.

Let me take a moment to explain. Most Christians will admit that Jesus was a "friend of sinners," but have you ever noticed that he never described himself that way. It was the religious community that put those labels on him. What's amazing about Jesus is that when He hung out with sinners, I truly think that He didn't act like they were sinners. Those words, "a friend of sinners," were spoken with an upturned nose and a self-righteous sneer.

And I am afraid that's the same phrase the church has adopted today, "Love the sinner, hate the sin." It's that same self-righteous sneer heard in the words of those who dragged the woman caught in adultery to Jesus. Remember the story told in John 8:1-11? 1 *Jesus returned to the Mount of Olives, 2 but early the next morning he was back again at the Temple. A crowd soon gathered, and he sat down and taught them. 3 As he was speaking, the teachers of religious law and the Pharisees brought a woman who had been caught in the act of adultery. They put her in front of the crowd. 4 "Teacher," they said to Jesus, "this woman was caught in the act of adultery. 5 The law of Moses says to stone her. What do you say?" 6 They were trying to trap him into saying something they could use against him, but Jesus stooped down and wrote in the dust with his finger.*

7 They kept demanding an answer, so he stood up again and said, "All right, but let the one who has never sinned throw the first stone!" 8 Then he stooped down again and wrote in the dust.

9 When the accusers heard this, they slipped away one by one, beginning with the oldest, until only Jesus was left in the middle of the crowd with the woman. 10 Then Jesus stood up again and said to the woman, "Where are your accusers? Didn't even one of them condemn you?" 11 "No, Lord," she said.

And Jesus said, "Neither do I. Go and sin no more."

After kneeling and drawing in the sand Jesus says to her, *"Where are your accusers? Didn't even one of them condemn you?" "No, Lord,"* she said. *"Neither do I. Go and sin no more."* Jesus could have said *"You're a sinner, but I love you anyways."* She knew she was a sinner. It was very obvious to her with the angry crowd collecting rocks on the way to see Jesus. I think a lot of people look at the story of the woman caught in adultery as Jesus simply telling her to go and live a moral life. When Jesus comes to her and says "Neither do I condemn you," those are really life changing and life saving words. All too often the Church (and myself) have been on the side of those with the rocks saying, "You deserve this punishment. You deserve to be demeaned and criticized. Why? Because we have these Bible verses on our side."

I think that the position God wants us to hold is to be like Jesus who says, *"Neither do I condemn you."* Most Christians I've experienced want to jump straight to *"go and sin no more"* as if we're responsible for the morality of those around us. What was the greatest commandment of Jesus? *"Love your neighbor."*

Whatever these deeds were, the Ephesians don't hate the individuals themselves but their wicked behavior. This is important. There is something to be learned here. The church at Ephesus took a stand against these men and their teachings and was commended for doing so. And again, we too need to take a stand against those who teach false doctrine. John finishes off his letter to Ephesians with this:

7"*Anyone with ears to hear must listen to the Spirit and understand what he is saying to the churches. To everyone who is victorious I will give fruit from the tree of life in the paradise of God.*"

Note the change from an appeal to the individual, "*Anyone with ears to hear,*" to the plural, "*understand what he is saying to the churches.*" This change broadens the appeal of each message to all the churches because the messages are representative and applicable to all of us.

Here, the Spirit of God, who is the Spirit of truth and the author and teacher of Scripture, is calling on us to evaluate and to respond to the things that need to be learned and applied in these messages. In other words, the Spirit of God is saying to each of us, "*It is not enough to have good intentions. You must follow through!*" To "*hear what the Spirit says*" means to really listen and respond to the Spirit of God.

"*To everyone who is victorious I will give fruit from the tree of life in the paradise of God.*"

Who are these people who are victorious? The answer is simple: Christians—true followers of Jesus Christ, those who have been born of the Spirit of God. 1 John 5:4, 5 says this:

"*4For whatever is born of God overcomes the world; and this is the victory that has overcome the world—our faith.*

5 *Who is the one who overcomes the world, but he who believes that Jesus is the Son of God?"*

So the overcomer in this passage refers to "faithful" believers who will be rewarded for their perseverance. In this context, the one who overcomes is able to "eat of the tree of life." This tree of life is mentioned 11 times in three different books of the Bible.

The first is in Genesis 2:9; 3:22-24. God planted the tree of life (a literal tree) in the Garden of Eden, next to the tree of the knowledge of good and evil. After they sinned by eating from the tree of the knowledge of good and evil, Adam and Eve were banished from the garden so that they would not eat from the tree of life, lest they live forever in their fallen state.

The second is in the Book of Proverbs. Here we see the tree of life used in a figurative sense (Proverbs 3:18). The last reference is in Revelation 22:2, where it refers to a literal tree, so the tree of life is reserved for those over-comers who will rule and reign as co-heirs with Christ.

So the church is to be a visible expression of the love of God, who is not here in person. You see the one thing God intended to set His followers apart from all the other religions of the world was love. Listen to the words of Jesus in John 17:23: *"I am in them and you in me.*

Then they might be perfected (mature) *in this oneness* (unity) . . . *that the world will know that you sent me and that you love them as much as you love me."* NIV

"They will know we are Christians by our love, by our love. Yes, they will know that we are Christians by our love."

Notice that being perfected, being mature is reflected in love and unity and not in doctrinal distinctiveness. Do you see what is being said here? The only way this godless world will ever believe that Jesus is real is by seeing the church as a place that loves, cares, restores and accepts. So what the world needs now is. . .

God's love, shown through you and me.

Questions for Thoughtful Discussion

1. Do you agree with the statement that Christians in the United States today are unloving? Explain your answer.

2. On a scale of 1-10, with 1 being never and 10 being all the time, how would you describe your love for God according to Luke 10:27? Can you back up your answer with examples from your life?

3. Are you a patient person? Are there examples in your life where you have patiently persevered?

4. Are you able to discern who are the more popular false teachers are today? Why do you think Christians tolerate false teaching? Is it wrong to tolerate and follow someone who is known for their heretical teaching? Why?

5. Do you love Jesus? How would people know that you love Jesus? Would your actions show it?

6. Are you obedient to God's Word? What are some of the verses in Scripture that are hard for you to obey? Can you be disobedient and still call yourself a Christian?

7. How are you doing in the area of repentance? When was the last time you noticed the Spirit of God working in your life?

8. Jesus said that the most important commandments are "You shall love the Lord thy God with all your heart, all your soul, all your strength, and all you mind" and "You shall love your neighbor as yourself." He also said to his disciples, "A new commandment I give to you, that you love one another: just as I have loved you, you also are to love one another. By this all people will know that you my disciples, if you have love for one another." This is what is to define us as Christians: our love for God and, consequently, for one another and for our neighbors. The church, which is Christ's representative on Earth, is supposed to be the most loving group of people in the world.

So why isn't it? Do you have any ideas on how to act out God's love to others?

Chapter 3

THE CHURCH AT SMYRNA —
Faithful Until Death

In 2005 I made a trip to Dmitrovgrad, Russia to help out the only evangelical church in a city of over 200,000 people. Being a cold-war kid, I was very nervous about going to Russia. Even though it has been more than 20 years since the fall of the communist Soviet Union, I wasn't sure what to expect. After all, surely there was a good reason as to why President Reagan referred to Russia as the "Evil Empire." To my surprise, we had no issues entering the country and I immediately fell in love with the people. Before we boarded the train for Dmitrovgrad, we spent several days enjoying the sites of Moscow. As we were touring the Kremlin, I asked our tour guide if she could introduce me to a communist. She laughed and said that it is nearly impossible to find a communist in Russia today. I was surprised by her comment. During the whole trip not one person that I talked to would admit to ever being a communist.

When we got off the train after the 15-hour train ride to Dmitrovgrad it was Sunday morning. The pastor checked our passports into the city administration without any problems, or so I thought. Then it was off to the church for the Sunday morning service. The plan was for me to give the sermon that morning. I was really excited to have the chance to share God's Word with my brothers and sisters in Christ. I was even going to have an interpreter . . . how cool was that?

A few minutes before the service was to start, Pavel, who was the pastor, let me know that city officials had informed him that it was OK for me to preach, but I was not allowed mention anything concerning the Gospel of Jesus Christ in my message. I was going to laugh, but when I saw the serious look on his face I got the sense that he wasn't kidding. He wasn't. He continued by telling me that if they discovered that I had disobeyed, I could be arrested along with the rest of the team. I asked Pavel, "I thought the communists were pretty much out of the picture." Pavel replied, "It is not the communists that are the problem, it is the Russian Orthodox Church." I couldn't believe my ears . . . the Russian Orthodox Church? Yep . . . I had heard Pavel correctly. The Russian Orthodox Church was now the "heavy" against the spread of Christianity in Russia.

At this point Pavel asked the team, "So, what are you going to do?" Being very concerned at this point I asked Pavel, "What would happen to us if we were arrested?"

He told us that they would probably detain use for several hours and make us pay a hefty fine. Good, no torture or firing squad.

At this point the team and I decided that I would go ahead and preach my message as planned. Throughout the whole church service I was waiting for the local police to break in and drag my butt off to jail. It never happened. We endured several verbal threats during our week of ministry in Dmitrovgrad, but that was pretty much the extent of it.

All this to say that even though we were threatened with arrest for taking the Gospel of Jesus Christ to the people in Dmitrovgrad, that incident is ridiculously small compared to what believers are enduring throughout the rest of world.

Now persecution is nothing new to followers of Christ. As a matter of fact we are told to expect it. From verbal harassment to hanging, persecution for professing faith in Christ is as old as Christianity itself. The Jews persecuted Jesus Himself while he was walking the earth. His followers were tortured and executed for their faith. If you want to learn about Christians being tortured and killed for their faith, just pick up a copy of "**Foxe's Book of Martyrs**" sometime. It is a very sobering read.

Even today as I am writing this, there are believers around the world, who are being persecuted, imprisoned, tortured and even being beheaded because of their faith in Jesus Christ. It is estimated that nearly 100 million Christians are being persecuted around the world today. [34]

Peter tells us that testing and trials are apart of the Christian life.

9 *"Remember that your Christian brothers and sisters all over the world are going through the same kind of suffering you are. 10 In his kindness God called you to share in his eternal glory by means of Christ Jesus. So after you have suffered a little while, he will restore, support, and strengthen you, and he will place you on a firm foundation."*

1 Peter 5:9-10

It is in 2 Thessalonians that Paul reminds believers of their suffering and how their suffering will make them worthy of His Kingdom.

3 *"Dear brothers and sisters, we can't help but thank God for you, because your faith is flourishing and your love for one another is growing. 4 We proudly tell God's other*

churches about your endurance and faithfulness in all the persecutions and hardships you are suffering. 5 And God will use this persecution to show his justice and to make you worthy of his Kingdom, for which you are suffering." 2 Thessalonians 1:3-5

As you can see from these verses, and maybe from personal experience, persecution, hardships and suffering are a part of the Christian life.

Why are we discussing persecution? Because persecution is the theme of the letter to the church in Smyrna. Let's take a look at the city of Smyrna in the early first century.

The name Smyrna literally means "myrrh." Myrrh is an aromatic resin of a small thorny tree. It has been used throughout history as a perfume, incense and medicine (It was one of the gifts brought by the Magi to the child Jesus). Smyrna was a beautiful, rich and prosperous city, forty miles north of Ephesus, on the Aegean Sea at the mouth of the small river Meles. The city had a good harbor and was one of the chief highways to the interior of Asia Minor. Because of its location it had become a popular trading-center. The city was built at the head of a gulf that reached some 30 miles inland. The outer harbor was used as a place for the mooring of large ships. The inner harbor was small enough that it could be closed to the seagoing boats by simply drawing a chain across the harbor.

The population of Smyrna at the time of John's writing was probably around 250,000 people. In Roman times, Smyrna was considered the most brilliant city of Asia Minor, successfully rivaling Pergamos and Ephesus. Smyrna was celebrated for its schools of science and medicine, and for many of its elaborate buildings. There was a hill named Mount Pagos. Around the crest of that hill a number of pagan temples had been erected forming a rough circle. Thus the name "the Crown of Asia."[35] On the slope of Mount Pagos was a theater, which seated 20,000 spectators. At the time it was the largest theater in Asia Minor. The Olympian games had been celebrated there.

The Smyrna streets were wide and paved. It was home to one of the most famous streets in the world at that time. It was called the "street of gold." I am not sure if the street was actually paved with gold, but this famous street began at the temple of Zeus and ended at the temple of Cybele. Smyrna was loaded with pagan worship to false gods in the first century. As mentioned earlier, there were many temples dedicated to pagan gods built in the city.

Here is a list of a few of them:

Zeus: In Greek mythology Zeus was the king of the gods, the ruler of Mount Olympus, and the god of the sky and thunder. This is where the Olympian games were celebrated. The Romans worshipped Zeus as Jupiter.

Athena: She was believed to be the daughter of Zeus and was an armed warrior goddess, and appears in Greek mythology as a helper of many heroes.

Emperor Tiberius: In 23 AD a temple was built in Smyrna in honor of Tiberius and his mother Julia, on the Golden Street, connecting the temples of Zeus and Cybele. Tiberius reigned as Roman emperor in imperial Rome after Augustus from 14 AD to 37 AD.

Cybele: Was the particular favorite of emperor Augustus. Cybele represented the fertile Earth, a goddess of nature and of wild animals.

Some of the more recent archaeological discoveries in old Smyrna have revealed the statues of Hermes, Hestia, Dionysus, Eros and Hercules. Speaking of god's, one of the more popular was Dionysus, the god of wine and moral debauchery. There is a well-known statue in ancient Smyrna called "The Drunk Old Woman" which illustrates the prevalent habits of the population.[36]

While this is not an exhaustive list of pagan worship in Smyrna, it is sufficient to demonstrate the level of false worship that the Christians of the time were up against.

Smyrna had a large Jewish population who were rightly proclaiming the one true and living God, but had rejected Jesus Christ as the Messiah. In addition to the persecution of the Romans, the Christians also faced Jewish persecutions, which were considerable.

So, what about the Church in Smyrna? The Church in Smyrna probably originated within the large Jewish colony located there. Interestingly enough Smyrna is never mentioned anywhere in the book of Acts.

We can assume that the church was probably started sometime during Paul's three years in Ephesus. We know from his ministry in Ephesus there was a great harvest that extended far beyond that city. In fact, it says that all who lived in Asia heard the Word of the Lord, both Jews and Greeks (Acts 19:10) So there was a tremendous proclamation of the Gospel going on.

Three major names are affiliated with Smyrna. They are the Apostle John, Polycarp, who was a bishop and martyr, and Irenaeus, who was an early church Father and apologist. It is here in Smyrna that Irenaeus first heard Polycarp as a boy. Irenaeus was probably a native of Smyrna. After the second fall of Jerusalem in 135 AD, it became more universally recognized that the successor of the Apostle John was Polycarp.

Polycarp was a pupil of John, and a prominent leader in the church of Smyrna. It was here that Polycarp suffered martyrdom in AD 155 (More about him in a minute).

We do know that, for this little church in Smyrna, life was dangerous.

The Ephesians worshipped the goddess Artemis and those in Smyrna worshipped Caesar. As early as 26 A. D., during the reign of Tiberius Caesar, a temple had been erected to the emperor, and thus the Christians of Smyrna were confronted with the need to annually to choose between saying, "Jesus is Lord," or, "Caesar is Lord." That was the test the Romans applied to all their citizens.

It meant that a great deal of pressure and persecution came upon this church because of their unwillingness to bow to Caesar.

Some of the most severe persecution came during the reign of Emperor Domitian. Under his rule many Christians suffered the most dreadful torments. They were put to death at the stake, or by wild beasts in the amphitheater; their properties confiscated by the empire, they were often enslaved, abused and tortured; and the only test applied to them was whether they would throw a few grains of incense into the fire as a sacrifice to the Roman emperor, or whether they would refuse.

And if that wasn't bad enough, the Jewish population likewise despised the Christians and would frequently turn them into the Roman authorities as conspirators against the emperor for refusing to bow down to worship him.

As I mentioned earlier, John had a disciple named Polycarp who was a prominent Christian leader in Smyrna. Polycarp was probably 25-30 years old when John died. Polycarp himself lived until he was martyred around 156 AD in Smyrna. According to history he was tied to a stake in the amphitheater, pierced through the heart by a Roman soldier and then burned in front of an audience of tens of thousands of Romans screaming for his death.

Persecution was a way of life for the believers in Smyrna. Understanding what these early believers went through can help us clearly understand Jesus message to them.

By the way the city is still in existence today. It is the modern city of Izmir and home to some 400,000 people. [37] It's interesting to note that although it is in Turkey, which is an Islamic nation, it is predominantly a Christian city. Of the seven cities mentioned in Revelation only Smyrna has had a continual Christian influence since the first century.

Let's look at Jesus letter to the persecuted believers in the city of Smyrna.

8 *"Write this letter to the angel of the church in Smyrna. This is the message from the one who is the First and the Last, who was dead but is now alive:"*

If you look closely at these seven churches, Smyrna and Philadelphia are the only two churches in which Jesus has nothing negative to say. So in this letter there will be no chastisement from the Lord. We have already discussed in the previous chapter who the "messenger" could possibly be.

Notice how the Lord reveals himself to them in this letter. He says, *"I am the First and the Last. I am the one who was dead but is now alive."*

Notice the extremes: First and last; death and life. Jesus presents himself as the Lord of the extremes. He is the proverbial bookend; there is nothing before him and nothing behind him. He holds everything in between. He is in total control.

If you look in the book of Isaiah, you will also see that God calls Himself the First and Last (Isaiah 41:4, Isaiah 43:10, Isaiah 44:6 and 48:12). Here that same title is used to designate Jesus Christ. You will see this in Revelation chapter 1 verse 17, again in chapter 2 verse 8, and once again in chapter 22 and verse 13. Jesus Christ is the eternal infinite God, already in existence when all things were created. He is the last, and He will go on forever. When other things cease, He does not.

And then He referred Himself as the One who was dead but is now alive.

Why does Jesus designate Himself this way to this fellowship of believers? I believe it is because of their persecution. Jesus is saying to them, life is tough for you; it's hard living in this world. I just want you to know that I was here before it started and I'll be here after it's over. I transcend all of this and so do you because of your relationship to Me.

Furthermore, I know about dying for I was dead . . . literally I became dead . . . and yet I've been resurrected. And so He reminds them that even should they die in the persecution, they'll not experience anything He hasn't experienced.

Should they die, they will not be cut off from His eternal resurrection power. No matter what you're going through, I have been there. The Lord Jesus suffered the most unjust, the most severe, persecution and death. He suffered death on a cross bearing the sins of the world. That is the supreme suffering.

Jesus wasn't just some guy offering flippant advice. In fact, His opening words to them in verse 9 were, "*I know about your suffering.*" The Greek word that was used here is very significant. The Greek word is *oida*. *Oida* suggests fullness of "knowledge." It was a shared experience. It wasn't just a "yeah, I know how you must feel." Jesus is saying "I was there." He had full knowledge of what they were going through. That is the message of Jesus to the believers at Smyrna, and that goes for us as well.

Let's look at Jesus commendation to them in verse 9-10:

9 *"I know about your suffering and your poverty—but you are rich! I know the blasphemy of those opposing you. They say they are Jews, but they are not, because their synagogue belongs to Satan. 10 Don't be afraid of what you are about to suffer. The devil will throw some of you into prison to test you. You will suffer for ten days. But if you remain faithful even when facing death, I will give you the crown of life."*

He says I know your tribulation (*thlipsis*). I know the pressure you're under. *"Thlipsis"* is the Greek word for pressure. It primarily means "a pressing, pressure." This word was actually used in the classical Greek to describe someone who would be lying on the ground and then stoned to death. It conveys intense and constant pressure that often leads to death.

These Christians in Smyrna knew suffering—they were under intense pressure. They had something in common with the believers in Hebrews 11.

35 *" . . . But others were tortured, refusing to turn from God in order to be set free. They placed their hope in a better life after the resurrection. 36 Some were jeered at, and their backs were cut open with whips. Others were*

93

chained in prisons. 37 Some died by stoning, some were sawed in half, and others were killed with the sword. Some went about wearing skins of sheep and goats, destitute and oppressed and mistreated. 38 They were too good for this world, wandering over deserts and mountains, hiding in caves and holes in the ground." Hebrews 11:35-38

To these believers in Smyrna, suffering was to be their "lot in life." Not only were they presently suffering; Jesus tells them that they would continue to suffer in the future. These believers in Smyrna faced the dilemma of having to submit to human authority (Rom 13:1-7; 1 Pet 2:13-17), but not at the expense of disobeying God (Acts 5:29).

There is a constant tension between those two relationships. Followers of Christ are asked to submit to unbelieving authorities, but not to obey that which violates the clearly revealed will of God. Where will the Church draw the line between obeying the government and following God? It is something we will need to start considering.

So not only did the believers in Smyrna have pressure from the Roman government and the Jews, but there was economical pressure as well. "*I know about your poverty (but you are rich).*" Materially, the believers in Smyrna were destitute, probably because they insisted on worshipping Christ. Evidently their persecutors were cutting off some of their incomes or making it hard for them to find jobs. There are two Greek words for poor. One of the words is *penes,* which basically means you have nothing superfluous, you're not wealthy, you just have enough to satisfy your basic needs. That's not the word used here. The word used is *penichros*, which means you have nothing at all, absolute poverty, and complete destitution.

There is a good possibility that many of the believers in Smyrna might have been slaves. These followers of Christ were poor because of their faith. They had been robbed and plundered, slandered, accused, and even imprisoned. This church had every human reason to collapse.

There is a cost to following Christ. Here in America, there is some religious persecution, but it is very subtle, at least for now! Why? Because it is still pretty much a free country and many Christians are not witnessing or taking a strong stand for Christ. I wonder how many "Christians" here in the states would follow Christ if it cost them financially. How would you react if you lost your job and financial stability because you were a follower of Jesus? How would you support you family? It is something to think about.

What does Jesus mean by "but you are rich?" Well, how about that they were rich positionally?

Look at Ephesians 1:3-8.

3 *All praise to God, the Father of our Lord Jesus Christ, who has blessed us with every spiritual blessing in the heavenly realms because we are united with Christ. 4 Even before he made the world, God loved us and chose us in Christ to be holy and without fault in his eyes. 5 God decided in advance to adopt us into his own family by bringing us to himself through Jesus Christ. This is what he wanted to do, and it gave him great pleasure. 6 So we praise God for the glorious grace he has poured out on us who belong to his dear Son. 7 He is so rich in kindness and grace that he purchased our freedom with the blood of his Son and for- gave our sins. 8 He has showered his kindness on us, along with all wisdom and understanding.*

Peter takes this to a practical level.

14 *"But even if you suffer for doing what is right, God will reward you for it. So don't worry or be afraid of their threats. 15 Instead, you must worship Christ as Lord of your life. And if someone asks about your Christian hope, always be ready to explain it. 16 But do this in a gentle and respectful way. Keep your conscience clear. Then if people speak against you, they will be ashamed when they see what a good life you live because you belong to Christ. 17 Remember, it is better to suffer for doing good, if that is what God wants, than to suffer for doing wrong!"*
1 Peter 3:14-17

12 *"Dear friends, don't be surprised at the fiery trials you are going through, as if something strange were happening to you.* 13 *Instead, be very glad—for these trials make you partners with Christ in his suffering, so that you will have the wonderful joy of seeing his glory when it is revealed to all the world.*

14 *So be happy when you are insulted for being a Christian for then the glorious Spirit of God rests upon you."* 1 Peter 4:12-14

These are some great truths we should memorize and apply to our lives. Look again at the last part of verse 9:

"I know the blasphemy of those opposing you. They say they are Jews, but they are not, because their synagogue belongs to Satan."

The word "blasphemy" means to slander or speaking against. The slander that the Smyrna believers were enduring came from Jews who were particularly antagonistic toward Christians.

"They say they are Jews but they are not." Now that poses the question, were they really Jews? And the answer from a physical standpoint, is yes. And so, these were Jews in the physical sense but not true Jews. Look at what Paul writes about them in Romans.

28 *"For you are not a true Jew just because you were born of Jewish parents or because you have gone through*

the ceremony of circumcision. 29 No, a true Jew is one whose heart is right with God. And true circumcision is not merely obeying the letter of the law; rather, it is a change of heart produced by God's Spirit." Romans 2:28,29

So in that sense though physically Jewish they are spiritually pagan. It is like Americans who think that they are Christian just because they have been born and raised in the United States. These Smyrna believers were being mercilessly slandered at the mouths and hands of these Jews. They joined with the Romans in putting Christians to death as they came together to stamp out Christianity. You need to understand that the hatred of the Jews for Christians is a familiar fact to anybody who reads the book of Acts.

For example, if you read in Acts chapter 13 and verse 50, you see hatred for the believers in Antioch. If you read chapter 14 verses 2 and 5 you'll see their hatred for Christians expressed in Iconium. You see the Jews hatred for Christians in the city of Lystra described in chapter 14 verse 19. Again in chapter 17 verse 5 you see their hatred against the church in Thessalonica. They not only rejected Christ and persecuted Him on the cross, but they went after His followers. Everywhere Paul went the Judaizers chased him.

This type of hostile treatment leads Jesus to call these people "a synagogue of Satan." Jesus was very "in your face" when it came to dealing with false teachers, Pharisees and the likes. This persecution that the believers in Smyrna were going thru was going to continue. Look at verse 10:

10 *"Don't be afraid of what you are about to suffer. The devil will throw some of you into prison to test you. You will suffer for ten days. But if you remain faithful even when facing death, I will give you the crown of life."*

Jesus is telling them, "guess what . . . the suffering is going to continue but do not fear." Luke tells us: 4 *"Dear friends, don't be afraid of those who want to kill your body; they cannot do any more to you after that. 5 But I'll tell you whom to fear. Fear God, who has the power to kill you and then throw you into hell. Yes, he's the one to fear."* Luke 12:4,5

The apostle Paul writes in Romans 8:18: *"Yet what we suffer now is nothing compared to the glory he will reveal to us later."*

Peter writes: *"But even if you suffer for doing what is right, God will reward you for it. So don't worry or be afraid of their threats."* 1 Peter 3:14

Jesus tells us in Matthew: *"Don't be afraid of those who want to kill your body; they cannot touch your soul.*

99

Fear only God, who can destroy both soul and body in hell."
Matthew 10:2

Get the message? Don't be afraid of those who want to kill your body; they cannot touch your soul.

Fear only God, who can destroy both soul and body in hell. Let me give you some hope . . . if you have not suffered as of yet, cheer up, you will . . . it is coming. How can I say that? Look at 2 Timothy 3:12.

"Yes, and everyone who wants to live a godly life in Christ Jesus will suffer persecution."

The Gospel of John tells us: 18 *"If the world hates you, remember that it hated me first. 19 The world would love you as one of its own if you belonged to it, but you are no longer part of the world. I chose you to come out of the world, so it hates you . . . 20 Since they persecuted me, naturally they will persecute you. "* John 15:18-20

Jesus goes on to tell them they will not only suffer for their faith, but some of them will be imprisoned.

" . . . You will suffer for ten days. But if you remain faithful even when facing death, I will give you the crown of life."

What does he mean by ten days?" Doesn't sound like a very long sentence to me. Some theologian's think it means ten years, in that John is using a day as if it were a year. Some think it means just an undetermined amount of time. I think that when John said ten days, he probably means ten days. I don't try to read anything into this. Could this be a Roman judicial sentence for a specific crime in that day? Possibly.

John probably intended us to interpret this period as a 10 literal 24-hour day that lay in the near future of the original recipients of this letter. There is nothing in the text that provides a clue that we should take this number in a figurative sense; however, it would seem that the emphasis falls on the fact that the Lord limits the testing. Just as Satan was given permission to test Job, within limits, so Satan was allowed to tests the saints of Smyrna, but for a specific period of time.

But here is the point I want for you to understand. Notice the words, "*So that you may be tested.*"

God could very well be saying, "Go ahead Satan . . . have at them." Why? Because Jesus could saying, "Hey, you belong to Me and I still have reign over you." Why would I say that? Remember in the book of Job God allowed Satan to test Job, but he couldn't physically harm him?

12"*All right, you may test him," the LORD said to Satan. "Do whatever you want with everything he possesses, but don't harm him physically." So Satan left the LORD's presence.* Job 1:12.

I believe the same thing could be happening here. Remember the conversation between Peter and Jesus in Luke chapter 22? Jesus looks at Peter and He says: 31*"Simon, Simon, Satan has asked to sift you like wheat. 32 But I have pleaded in prayer for you, Simon, that your faith should not fail"*

How do you think Peter responded to that statement? If I were Peter, I would have asked Jesus, *"Well Lord, you did tell Satan no, didn't you?"* That would have definitely been my argument. But God does this for a reason. I believe this was a direct message to Satan to prove that God is still on the throne and in charge. Satan was after Peter but Jesus said, *"I have pleaded in prayer for you, Simon, that your faith should not fail."*

Even though Peter failed miserably by denying Jesus 3 times, he was later restored and was eventually martyred for his faith.

I believe that on a supernatural level, God and Satan are engaged in a battle over God's faithful. And Satan is constantly trying to defeat and destroy us. And God says, *"All right, go ahead and give it a try. "*

So what do we need to take away from this? That God is in complete control of your circumstances. He always knows what's happening. Yet, He does refrain from intervening in certain circumstances because He has a purpose in our tribulation, our trials, our poverty, and the slander that comes against Christians (see Matt 5:11-12; Rom 5:3-5; Jas 1:2-4; 1 Pet 1:6-7). God uses trials to fine-tune our character for His glory. He uses trials either as a barbell (to steadily strengthen) or a blowtorch (to burn away).

Let me ask you, when you face trials and problems, is your immediate response a plea for instant relief? Or is your overriding realization recognition that God has sovereignly designed these circumstances as a means to deepen your relationship with Him. Let me suggest memorizing a verse that I just learned this week.

"I want to know Christ and experience the mighty power that raised him from the dead. I want to suffer with him, sharing in his death, so that one way or another I will experience the resurrection from the dead!" Philippians 3:10,11

Suffering for Christ was and is a privilege, not a sorrow . . . not a mistake. Although your trials may seem severe at the time, know that God's grace is sufficient to carry you through any trial. And if your suffering ends in death, know that a great reward is awaiting you. Scottish soldier and clergyman George F. MacLeod once said:

"The greatest criticism of the American church today is that no one wants to persecute it: because there is nothing very much to persecute it about," [38]

Now Jesus gives His final council to the believers in Smyrna. Look at the last part of verse 10-11. " . . . *But if you remain faithful even when facing death, I will give you the crown of life.* 11 *Anyone with ears to hear must listen to the Spirit and understand what he is saying to the churches. Whoever is victorious will not be harmed by the second death."*

Jesus is simply saying, if your faith is real, and you're faithful until the end, then I will give you life, the crown that is life. This crown of life appears to be like a victor's *stephanos* crown, given for enduring the trials and tests of life, even to the point of death, without denying Christ.

Jesus is saying, "I do not require you to be successful; I require you to be faithful." James 1:12 tells us: "*God blesses those who patiently endure testing and temptation. Afterward they will receive the crown of life that God has promised to those who love him.*"

Jesus is simply saying, "If you listen to what this letter is saying to you, if you trust me in times of suffering, tribulation and persecution, I will give you the gift of eternal life and you will have nothing to fear from the judgment of God."

It is what Paul rejoices about in Romans 8, when he starts the chapter with "*There is now no condemnation for those who belong to Christ Jesus.*" And then he finishes chapter 8 with these great words:

38 " . . . *And I am convinced that nothing can ever sep-arate us from God's love. Neither death nor life, neither angels nor demons, neither our fears for today nor our worries about tomorrow—not even the powers of hell can separate us from God's love.* 39 *No power in the sky above or in the earth below—indeed, nothing in all creation will ever be able to separate us from the love of God that is revealed in Christ Jesus our Lord."* Romans 8:38b-39

Norman Vincent Peale once said: "*The only people who don't have problems are those who live in cemeteries.*"[39]

We all have problems. None of us are immune to that fact. The good news is that Jesus knows all about our troubles and trials. Nothing escapes Him, and He has already experienced them all. His very words to us should comfort us: "Be faithful, and fear not." Are you unfaithful and fearful? Are you feeling that life's pressures are too much to bear? Well Jesus has a message for you - it is the letter to all those who suffer. Three things you need to remember:

1) Jesus says, "I knows what you are suffering and I can sympathize because I've been there."

2) Jesus says you do not have to be afraid, because I have everything under control. Nothing happens to you without first going through Me.

3) Finally He says, "If you stand firm, I will give you a reward – not only will you have eternal life but you will also receive a crown of life."

It has been said, "*A person is not prepared to live until he is prepared to die.*" Are you ready to die for Christ? If He privileged you to suffer to that extent, would you be willing?

In closing, John again writes: "*He who has an ear let him hear what the Spirit says to the churches.*"

Questions for Thoughtful Discussion

1. Have you ever faced any type of persecution for your faith in Jesus Christ? If so, how did you respond?

2. Have you learned to patiently endure? How do you react when it seems that life is against you such as illness, financial troubles, temptation, persecution or tough people? Do you see it as God's plan for your life?

3. In your own words, what does it mean to you to be victorious? How would this look in the areas of spiritual conflict?

4. The early Christians faced persecution from the Jews. Have you ever had another believer turn against you or slander you? How did you deal with it. Do you agree with the statement that Christians "shoot their wounded?"

Chapter 4

THE CHURCH AT PERGAMUM —
Life in the Shadow of Satan

There is a story of a New York family that bought a ranch out West where they intended to raise cattle. Friends visited and asked if the ranch had a name. *"Well,"* said the would-be cattleman, *"I wanted to name it the Bar-J. My wife favored Suzy-Q. One son liked the Flying-W, and the other wanted the Lazy-Y. So we're calling it the Bar-J-Suzy-Q-Flying-W-Lazy-Y."*

"But where are all your cattle?" the friends asked.

"Well," the cattleman said, *"None survived the branding."*

Compromise, it can be either good or bad. In the case of the family, the father compromised and got a name that pleased everyone. In the case of the cattle, the compromise didn't turn out in their favor.

This chapter is about compromise. More specific, it is about the compromising Church. Just as the Church at

Pergamum made compromises with its culture in the first century, the same can be said for the Church today. The findings in numerous national polls conducted by highly respected pollsters such as the Gallup Organization and the Barna Group are simply shocking. Evangelical theologian Michael Horton says, *"Gallup and Barna hand us survey after survey demonstrating that evangelical Christians are as likely to embrace lifestyles every bit as hedonistic, materialistic, self-centered, and sexually immoral as the world in general."* [40]

George Barna puts it in plain simple language: *"Every day, the church is becoming more like the world it allegedly seeks to change."*[41]

He goes on to say, *"American Christianity has largely failed since the middle of the twentieth century because Jesus' modern-day disciples do not act like Jesus."*[42]

Another study conducted by The Roper Organization in 1990, found that the moral behavior of born again Christians actually worsened after their conversions.[43]

I am reminded of Jesus' warning to us in Matthew 5:13: *"You are the salt of the earth. But what good is salt if it has lost its flavor? Can you make it salty again? It will be thrown out and trampled underfoot as worthless."*

How can Christians be so *un*-Christ-like? Easy answer! They act un-Christ-like because they are not like Christ.

The Pew Research Center finds that the percentage of adults (ages 18 and older) who describe themselves as Christians has dropped by nearly eight percentage points in just seven years, from 78.4% in an equally massive Pew Research survey in 2007 to 70.6% in 2014. [44] Common sense would tell us that a lot of these people are not true believers.

How many true, evangelical, Bible-believing Christians are there in the United States? Would you believe somewhere around seven to eight percent.

Yep . . . you read that correctly, only about seven to eight percent of Americans are probably what you could consider a true follower in Christ Jesus.

In George Barna's 2011 book **Futurecast** he gives the probable number of evangelical Christians in his findings. According to Barna, "*about seven percent of the public can be considered evangelical Christians.*" [45]

How many Christians is that?

In John Dickerson's book (Which I highly recommend) **The Great Evangelical Recession**, John gives us a clear picture of where we evangelicals stand in reference to the numbers of unbelievers in the United States. John writes: "*Now, we have seen that in reality, the population of evangelical Christians in the United States is much smaller. It's actually about the population of New York State, around 22*

million. So now make New York State the 'evangelical' color,
and change every other state to the color on nonbelievers.
Picture all forty-nine of the other states as nonbelieving.
That is the reality of our size in the United States." [46]

Those are very sobering statistics, but if only a handful
of Christians on the Day of Pentecost could turn the world
upside down, then why not seven percent today?

So what do we know about the ancient city
of Pergamum?

The city of Pergamum is located about 49 miles north
of Smyrna and is set about 15 miles inland from the
Aegean coast. The ancient historian Pliny called it *"the*
most distinguished city in Asia Minor." [47]

Of all the cities of the seven churches, Pergamum is
the best preserved archeologically. The name Pergamum
has a dual meaning, having been the combination of two
Greek words, Pergos, and Gamos. There is quite a bit of
confusion as to the correct translation of this word. Some
commentators translate Pergamum as *"improper mar-*
riage." Other say it comes from the name of the parchment (*pergamene*) the Greeks made in the city. The other
common definition out there is "married to the tower."
Some say *pergos* could mean "tower or citadel" while
gamos means "married." So . . . take your pick. I can see
the parchment translation being possibly correct. I can

also go with the high tower or citadel translation. Why? Because the city of Pergamum was situated like a fortress atop a huge hill in the Valley of Caucus (Caicus River?). If you visited the area today you would find the present city of Bergama in Turkey.

In spite of its natural defenses, the city took the easy way out and surrendered quickly to Rome rather than be conquered. The city elders saw Rome's aggressive advance and realized that there was little hope of survival. So they offered their services to Rome and in return the city became the official Roman seat of government, the provincial capital of Asia Minor—sort of a quid pro quo. Later, the capital was eventually transferred to Ephesus.

Under the Emperor Hadrian, Pergamum was granted the title of metropolis and as a result, an ambitious building program was carried out: massive temples, a stadium, a theatre, a huge forum and an amphitheater that seated 10,000 were constructed.

Pergamum reached the height of its greatness under Roman Imperial rule and was home to about 200,000 inhabitants.

Pergamum was considered a religious city because it was overrun with pagan temples.

The city had so many Greek and Roman temples that the very presence of Satan seemed to have settled upon the city. That is probably why Jesus refers to Pergamum in our text as the city "where Satan lives."

Pergamum proudly boasted of having at least four great temples. They had a temple dedicated to Dionysus, the god of wine and drama; they had one for Athena, the goddess of wisdom in art and war; they had one for Asclepius the god of healing, and the biggest temple in town was dedicated to Zeus.

Zeus' massive temple was built on a hill overlooking the city and it was referred to as "Zeus' Throne." It was four stories high or about four times the size of the seat Lincoln sits on in the Lincoln Memorial. It would smoke all day long because of the sacrifices to Zeus. That smoke continually cast a shadow over the city.

The god of Asclepius, which I mentioned earlier, was the "god of healing." The symbol of this god was a snake entwined around a staff.

This image can still be seen today as the caduceus, or emblem of the medical profession.

A constant influx of people came to Pergamum to be healed of their diseases. They would sleep overnight (often drug induced) and report their dreams to a priest the following day. The physician would then prescribe a cure, often a visit to the baths or a gymnasium. Since snakes were sacred to Asclepius, they were often used in healing rituals. Non-venomous snakes were left to crawl on the floor in dormitories where the sick and injured slept. Tradition was that if a snake crawled over you, you would be eventually healed.

Once healed, patients would prostrate themselves before the statue of Asclepius, thanking him for their healing, and would often give him gifts. Finally, they would inscribe their name and the ailment from which they'd been cured on a large, white stone as a testimony to the god. The temple became so well known as a place of healing, it was later expanded into a lavish spa.

This Sanctuary of Asclepius grew in fame and was considered one of the most famous therapeutic and healing centers of the Roman world.

An interesting side-note: Priests would interview potential patients to determine whether they were acceptable for healing. Interestingly, they turned away people who were dying and women who were ready to deliver babies. They didn't want a particular patient's death to "taint" their god or their giving. This sounds a lot like the screening some of our faith healers today go through in picking out who makes it up to the stage to receive their "so-called" healing.

The city was also renowned for its temple to Caesar Augustus, the first temple ever built to honor a living emperor. Emperor worship was a big deal in Pergamum.

In other cities like Smyrna, you could burn your pinch of incense once a year and say, "Caesar is Lord" and then you could go on with life. In Pergamum, worshiping the emperors of Rome was 365 days a year. The main issue facing the believers in this city was a constant, daily pressure to deny Christ and worship the emperor as god.

Pergamum became famous for its invention of vellum, a writing material made from animal skins. This invention enhanced its library, which contained over 200,000 volumes. That is especially impressive when you realize that these library halls were filled with handwritten scrolls, not like the books that we have today.

Authors from all over were invited to contribute to the massive collection of writings, which was second only to the library of Alexandria.

There is a very interesting story related to the library at Pergamum. You see, for centuries if you wanted to write something you had to use papyrus. Papyrus was made from bulrushes that grow on the banks of the Nile. For a long time, Papyrus was one of Egypt's main exports.

In the third century BC the king of Pergamum was a guy named Eumenes and like his fellow "Pergamumites,"

Eumenes was very proud of his city—especially its library. What he wanted most was for his library to move from being the number two library in the world up to the number one slot. So he persuaded the man in charge of the library in Alexandria, a skilled librarian named Aristophanes, to agree to leave and come to work for him in Pergamum. Well, the ruler in Egypt at that time was Ptolemy and when he got wind of what was going on he put Aristophanes under lock and key. To punish Eumenes for attempting to steal his librarian, Ptolemy put an embargo in place on the export of papyrus to Pergamum.

So with this embargo in place, the scholars in Pergamum put their heads together to find a substitute for papyrus. And the result of their labors was parchment or vellum, which is made from the skins of animals. Parchment proved to be a far superior writing material and it eventually wiped out the papyrus market.

Legend has it that Mark Antony later gave Cleopatra all of the 200,000 volumes from the library at Pergamum for the Library at Alexandria as a wedding present. [48]

During the second half of the 3rd century Pergamum started to decline. The decline was due to an earthquake in 262 AD and the eventual sacking of the city by the Goths. The arrival of Christianity did not help stop the decline as the buildings, which had honored the pagan gods, were no longer considered desirable. Even the shrine to Asclepius was abandoned.

Interestingly, the book of Acts makes no mention of the founding of the church in Pergamum. According to Acts 16:7-8, Paul passed through the region of Mysia, where Pergamum was located, on his second missionary journey, but there is no record that Paul either preached the Gospel or founded a church there during that time. Most likely, Paul founded this church during his ministry at Ephesus (Acts 19:10) when the Gospel was preached throughout Asia.

This was the city of Pergamum. Jesus describes it as the city where "Satan has his throne." The church at Pergamum was surrounded by a pagan culture, just as we are surrounded by an increasingly godless culture. Let me ask you, do you ever feel like you are living in a city where Satan rules? When you watch the news and hear the headlines, does it seem as if Satan's having his way more often than not?

As you study this letter, be attentive to what God wants to teach you through His Word.

The believers in Pergamum had compromised so Jesus wrote them a very stinging letter in which He began with the words: *"Write this letter to the angel of the church in*

Pergamum. This is the message from the one with the two-edged sharp sword."

Jesus is literally saying to them I am the one with the "sword, the two edged (hyphen) sharp." It is a sharp, two-edged sword. That is pretty descriptive.

There are a few of words that He could have used for sword. One is a little bitty sword *machairan* like the sword Peter used on Malchus in John 18:10. Another term for sword is the word *rhomphaian*, which is warrior's broadsword. But the word used in this verse is *distomon*, which is a two- edged sword. It was about four feet long and was held by two hands. Both edges were razor sharp so you could swing it in both directions in order to clear a whole path of real estate in front of you. It was, of course, a sword used to kill in battle. That is the term used here.

Look at verse 13: *"I know that you live in the city where Satan has his throne, yet you have remained loyal to me. You refused to deny me even when Antipas, my faithful witness, was martyred among you there in Satan's city."*

In this verse Jesus mentions three things about the believers in Pergamum.

1. They lived in a city where "Satan has his throne." Some scholars think it refers to the great altar of Zeus, which was on the hillside overlooking the city.

The folks in Pergamum could look up at any time and see what Jesus calls "Satan's throne." Here is an interesting footnote of history: In the 1880's, a German archaeologist working in the city of Pergamum removed that throne from the hillside and took it to Europe. Today it can be seen in the Pergamum Museum in the city of Berlin.

2. They remained loyal to Him. The Greek literally says, "you hold fast." The Greek word is *krateis*, which means to "hold on firmly." Even though they lived where there was no shortage of false gods and occult practice, they remained firm in their faith.

3. He knew of their endurance under persecution. The believers in Pergamum were suffering for Christ. As a result, Antipas (who was one of their own) was martyred.

Yet, in spite of the grave danger of naming the name of Christ, the believers in Pergamum persevered in their faith, refusing to deny their Lord. Antipas means "against all." This godly man lived up to his name. We do not know much about this man, although he is said to be the first martyr under the Roman persecution in Asia. Tradition says that Antipas was roasted to death in a brazen bull that was heated to a white heat. We are called to witness for Christ with our lives and our lips. And above all we are called to be faithful.

It seems to me that what the church community today tries to do is recreate the world in a safe Christian atmosphere. In my opinion, that is why today in our culture we have Christian TV and radio instead of Christians infiltrating secular TV and radio and having an influence. That's why we have Christian music and Christian schools and Christian yellow pages and Christian dating services. But these verses are reminding us that this was never the intention of Jesus.

Believers were meant to be the preserving element of society. Jesus says we are to be the "salt of the earth." You can't do that if you exit from society. You can't be the light of the world if you have disappeared into your own holy ghetto. And so the church today has withdrawn from culture rather than engaging culture. This is so far from the intention of Jesus. He never encouraged an escape mentality. He never encouraged the church to construct its own safe version of the world. What exactly was Jesus' intention for the believer?

13 *"But now I come to You; and these things I speak in the world so that they may have My joy made full in*

themselves. 14 I have given them your word. And the world hates them because they do not belong to the world, just as I do not belong to the world. 15 I'm not asking you to take them out of the world, but to keep them safe from the evil one. 16 They do not belong to this world any more than I do. 17 Make them holy by your truth; teach them your word, which is truth. 18 Just as you sent me into the world, I am sending them into the world. 19 And I give myself as a holy sacrifice for them so they can be made holy by your truth." John 17:13-19

Jesus engaged His culture; He didn't hang out with the "holier than thou crowd." I don't know how many times I've had people tell me: "As a Christian we need to come out and be separate from the world!" (2 Corinthians 6:17) Most of the time this passage is taken out of context. Paul is not telling us to have nothing to do with the world. This passage is not telling us to retreat behind our "sanctified" church walls and have nothing to do with unbelievers.

So what is Paul saying to us in this passage? The word Paul used for "separate" has three different definitions.

One word Paul could have used was *"chorizo"* which speaks of physical separation as in a divorce. (Mark 10:9) A second word Paul could have used was *"apochorizo"* which describes a larger physical separation such as when Paul and Barnabas parted and went different ways. (Acts 15:39)

The third word that Paul uses here is the word *"aphorizo." Aphorizo* can be used both in a physical sense and also in a figurative way such as to "mark off others by boundaries" or to "render distinct."

For example Paul used this word to describe himself as "separated to the Gospel of God." (Romans 1:1) Paul was not physically removed from other people; but he was set aside as distinct and different.

Let me give you an illustration that I heard when I was taking a hermeneutics class at Western Seminary with late Dr. Earl Radmacher. Explaining this passage from Corinthians, Dr. Radmacher gave a great illustration of this thought of being separate. In a vegetable garden you can have rows of carrots, beets, lettuce, roses, squash and green beans. The roses of course are not a vegetable. So, it could be said that the roses are *aphorizo* distinct, different from the other vegetables in the garden. Make sense?

This separation does not mean segregation. To live a separated life does not mean that we have to separate ourselves from the world. I can be living for Christ and be different and still be in this world, but not of this world.

Christians are not supposed to opt out of this world. Opting out is in a direct conflict with the message of Jesus. So the bottom-line—be a witness and be faithful.

Now the message to the believers in Pergamum takes a negative turn. Jesus begins His rebuke the same way He did with the church at Ephesus. The only difference is instead of saying, "I have *this* against you," Jesus says, "I have a *few* things against you."

14*"But I have a few complaints against you. You tolerate some among you whose teaching is like that of Balaam, who showed Balak how to trip up the people of Israel. He taught them to sin by eating food offered to idols and by committing sexual sin. 15 In a similar way, you have some Nicolaitans among you who follow the same teaching."*

Okay, so what is Jesus talking about in this passage? The reference to Balaam and Balak goes back to the book of Numbers in the Old Testament. The name "Balaam" can be understood in Hebrew as meaning *"he who conquers or he who destroys the people."* You can read about Balaam in Numbers 25. Balaam was a false prophet who had been hired by Balak, the King of Moab, to curse Israel. The problem was that whenever he tried to do so, he found he could not. Every time he tried to curse them, words of blessing came out of his mouth. God would not let him curse his people. So, in order to achieve the end for which he had been hired, he paid beautiful maidens from Moab and Midian to parade before the young men of Israel, tempting them into sexual immorality. By using women who worshiped idols he introduced idol worship into the tribes of Israel.

Thus he corrupted and enticed them into sin. You need to understand something—it wasn't just a couple of guys. The book of Numbers tells us that 24, 000 guys said "count me in."

Here's the point. They couldn't be defeated from the outside so Balaam in his trickery got them from the inside. Balaam and his transgressions are even mentioned in the New Testament.

In 2 Peter 2:15-16 Peter is describing false teachers. He writes:

15 *"They have wandered off the right road and followed the footsteps of Balaam son of Beor, who loved to earn money by doing wrong. 16 But Balaam was stopped from his mad course when his donkey rebuked him with a human voice."*

And Jude makes a similar remark: *"Woe to them! They have taken the way of Cain; they have rushed for profit into Balaam's error; they have been destroyed in Korah's rebellion."* Jude 11

So then in Revelation, Jesus picks up on the theme of Balaam's trickery as well, identifying it as tempting people to sexual immorality and illicit participation in pagan things—specifically, eating meat sacrificed to idols. The believers in Pergamum allowed themselves to be compromised from within.

The practice and the teachings of Balaam are alive and well in the church today. Two major issues are within the church today: the practice of pornography and sexual immorality. How do we compromise today. Take for example the acceptance of "Christian" couples living together out of wedlock would be a counterpart to the teachings of Balaam. Christians today turn a blind eye at sexual immorality.

Here are a few statistics that are absolutely frightening:

- 52 percent of pastors said they have looked at porn within the last 30 days (Some surveys today say it is as high as 62 percent)

- 50 percent of Christian men in the church are addicted to pornography

- 23 percent of Christian women in the church struggle with a porn addiction

- 90 percent of 8-16 year-old kids have viewed pornography [49]

According to the 2014 State of Dating In America Survey:

- 61 percent of Christians feel it is OK to have sex before marriage as long as you are committed to the dating relationship.

- 56 percent of Christians feel that it is OK to live together before marriage [50]

These figures show how porn usage and sexual immorality has infiltrated the church today. Satan is not stupid. If he can't get in one door, he will try another. How many Christian leaders have to fall? How many families and relationships have to be ruined before we wake up and repent?

Listen to what Paul tells us in 1 Thessalonians 4:2-5:

2 *"For you remember what we taught you by the authority of the Lord Jesus. 3 God's will is for you to be holy, so stay away from all sexual sin. 4 Then each of you will control his own body and live in holiness and honor—5 not in lustful passion like the pagans who do not know God and his ways."*

That is the error of Balaam. Jesus describes their sin pretty clearly—eating food that was offered to idols and being involved in sexual immorality. Since we don't have to worry too much about eating food sacrificed to idols today . . . stay away from sexual immorality!

The second false teaching affecting the believers in Pergamum was that they were being seduced by the error of the Nicolaitans. It is not exactly clear who these Nicolaitans were, but we do know that they were causing trouble within the church.

Remember this name came up in our chapter on the church in Ephesus. What do we know about the Nicolaitans?

The name "Nicolaitans" is derived from the Greek word *nikolaos*, a compound of the words *nikos* and *laos*. The word *nikos* is the Greek word that means to conquer or to subdue. The word *laos* is the Greek word for the people. It is also where we get our word for laity. When these two words are compounded into one, they form the name Nicolas, which literally means one who conquers and subdues the people. It seems to suggest that the Nicolaitans were somehow conquering and subduing the people.

To be honest, there are volumes of material out there by theologians and historians, each describing their own theory and research on who these Nicolaitans were and what they did do to cause such a ruckus in the early church. But from our passage here, we are told that they were holding to the same two sins as Balaam . . . eating foods offered to idols and sexual immorality. Jesus says in verse 16:

"Repent, otherwise, I will come to you and fight against them with the sword of my mouth."

Five of the seven churches are called to repent (Smyrna and Philadelphia are exceptions). Biblical repentance involves changing one's mind in a way that affects some change in the person.

What does he mean by the "sword of my mouth?" I believe Jesus is talking about judgment. A few pages over to Revelation chapter 19 we see the second coming of Jesus who is returning to earth to fight the gathered armies of this world. In verse 21 we read:

"Their entire army was killed by the sharp sword that came from the mouth of the one riding the white horse."

This is a threat and a promise. Jesus doesn't wink at compromise. He doesn't say, "That's okay. I've got unlimited grace and unending forgiveness, so it doesn't matter how you live." The church has to deal with its sin or else Jesus will come and remove the lampstand from the church. Either the church will discipline its sinning members or else Jesus will come and make war with His sword. And no church wants to be on the short end of that sword.

The church in Pergamum stands in stark contrast to the church in Ephesus. Our Lord could commend the saints at Ephesus because they hated the deeds of the Nicolaitans (2:6), while the church at Pergamum was willing to let it go on unchallenged.

The believers in Pergamum probably did not participate in the ways of these two heretical groups. They remained steadfast in their faith but they tolerated the eating of foods sacrificed to idols and ignored sexual sin by not exercising church discipline. They shared in the guilt, which brought judgment.

The only remedy for the sin of compromise is to repent. Let me explain repentance one more time in case you forgot. The root word for repent is *metanoeó* which means to change one's mind or purpose. I like the definition of repent that I learned as a new believer. I was taught that to repent means to change your mind, stop walking in one direction . . . turn 180 degrees and start walking in the other direction. Repentance needs to be a daily practice of the believer. Every time we sin, we need to confess and repent. Notice the change in the pronouns from "you" to "them." The usage of both pronouns would refer to the entire church. The church cannot tolerate evil in any form.

17 *"Anyone with ears to hear must listen to the Spirit and understand what he is saying to the churches."*

Jesus again appeals to the individual for spiritual change. Then Jesus closes with two important blessings to the overcomer. *"To everyone who is victorious I will give some of the manna that has been hidden away in heaven."*

We have discussed in past chapters who were the "victorious ones." I'm not going to repeat it here. In the Old Testament, manna stood for God's faithfulness to provide and sustain His people through the wilderness wanderings. In place of leeks, melons, garlic, and onions, Jesus rained down corn flakes from heaven. As a memorial to God's faithfulness, a portion of the manna was placed in the Ark of the Covenant (Exodus 16:32-34; Hebrews 9:4) to remind them that God had supplied their needs in the wilderness. In my opinion, I believe this "hidden manna" represents Jesus Christ who is the "Bread of Life." John 6:48-51 tells us:

48 *"Yes, I am the bread of life! 49 Your ancestors ate manna in the wilderness, but they all died. 50 Anyone who eats the bread from heaven, however, will never die. 51 I am the living bread that came down from heaven. Anyone*

who eats this bread will live forever; and this bread, which I will offer so the world may live, is my flesh."

Jesus provides the spiritual sustenance for those who overcome. We will receive from Christ the blessing of heaven. Ephesians 1:3 promises: *"All praise to God, the Father of our Lord Jesus Christ, who has blessed us with every spiritual blessing in the heavenly realms because we are united with Christ."*

Jesus continues, *"And I will give to each one a white stone, and on the stone will be engraved a new name that no one understands except the one who receives it."*

"A white stone" can perhaps be a little difficult to understand. Some commentators interpret this white stone as representing the stones from the breastplate of the Urim and Thummim. Others say the white stone represents a diamond, which symbolizes God's gift of eternal life to the believer.

It can be understood in terms of a marriage ceremony. We husbands customarily give our wives a diamond ring as a symbol commitment, love and the covenant of our marriage vows. I personally don't think either of these interpretations is correct. I tend to fall into a different camp because it makes better sense to me. The Romans would award the winners of their athletic games with a white stone. This white stone would be engraved with their name and would serve as a ticket to admission to a special awards banquet. I think Christ will give those who overcome entrance into a victory celebration in heaven. This could be the feast mentioned in Matthew 8:10-11.

You may be asking what feast? After seeing the faith of the Roman Centurion, Jesus says to the surrounding crowd: *"I tell you the truth, I haven't seen faith like this in all Israel! And I tell you this, that many Gentiles will come from all over the world—from east and west—and sit down with Abraham, Isaac, and Jacob at the feast in the Kingdom of Heaven."*

This feast could also be a reference to the Wedding Feast of the Lamb mentioned in Revelation 19:7-9: 7 *"Let us rejoice and be glad and give the glory to Him, for the marriage of the Lamb has come and His bride has made herself ready."* 8 *It was given to her to clothe herself in fine linen, bright and clean; for the fine linen is the righteous acts of the saints.* 9 *Then he said to me, "Write, 'Blessed are those who are invited to the marriage supper of the Lamb.'"*

Jesus also says that a "new name" will be written on this white stone, which "no one knows but he who receives it." Throughout Scripture a person's name is significant. That's why God changes peoples' names so frequently. Abram's name was changed to Abraham (Genesis 17:1-8). Jacob, which means *supplanter*, was changed to

Israel, (Genesis 32:27-29). Simon became Peter (Matthew 16:13-19). In the same vein, the overcoming believer is promised a new name, which demonstrates the character of the overcomer or his new responsibilities or both. This name shows something of what God has accomplished in his or her life through a faithful walk with Christ.

The word "new" in this verse is the Greek word *"kainon"* it does not mean new in contrast to old, but new in the sense of different.

Whatever rewards await the one who overcomes, I do know this:

" . . . No eye has seen, no ear has heard, and no mind has imagined what God has prepared for those who love him." 1 Corinthians 2:9

Questions for Thoughtful Discussion

1. Have you ever compromised in your spiritual life? How about at work, school or home?

2. What are some of the ways the Church compromises with the world?

3. Would you say that your lifestyle is more godly or worldly? If you are worldly, how would you go about changing it?

4. Does it concern you that in today's society, there is no difference in the behavior or lifestyle of a follower of Jesus and an unbeliever? Why is that?

5. Were you surprised by the statistic that only seven to eight percent of the people in the United States are Christian? Do you think with that small percentage of believers we can still make an impact for Christ in our community?

6. What are some ways in which we can engage our culture for Christ?

7. Are you shocked by the statistics of sexual immorality in the Church? How are you doing in staying sexually pure in your life?

8. How much of your churches ministry takes place outside of the church in your community?

9. Is repentance a daily practice in your life?

10. Do you feel pressured by the culture in which you live? What are some pressures that you have previously faced or are currently facing?

11. Do you understand to how to apply 2 Corinthians 6:17 to your life?

12. The definition of the word Nicolaitan is "one who conquers or subdues the people." Some believe that an additional sin needs to be added to sexual immorality and eating food to idols. That addition would be that of the priest ruling over the laity.

    During the third century we see the rise of priest and bishop beginning to rule over the laity. Do you see this as being an issue in the church today? Are pastors and elders ruling over the people? Is that the function of pastor and elder in the early church?

Chapter 5

THE CHURCH AT THYATIRA —
"To Be More Tolerant Than God"

A jo is the "nowhere" of Arizona.

At the turn of the 20th century, the city was known as the copper capital of the world for its high-grade ore. Ajo thrived for years, and at one time it was home to the largest copper company in the United States. Phelps Dodge ran the copper mine with over 1000 men working the mines.

Today, Ajo is basically the "gateway" to Rocky Point (Puerto Penasco) Mexico. People stop there to use the bathroom, grab some grub and gas up before heading to Mexico and visa versa. Other than being the brunt of jokes, Ajo is now home to mainly retired people, and the local Border Patrol agents and their families.

The next church we are going to look at is Thyatira. Like Ajo, Thyatira was "nowhere" Asia Minor. It wouldn't make much of a first impression. The city was 40 miles Southeast of Pergamum in the fertile Lycus River valley. It was graciously called "the Gateway to Pergamum." Little is known of its history beyond the fact that it once belonged to the kingdom of Pergamum. Very few archaeological remains have been found.

Thyatira was described as a citadel city. Sounds pretty impressive. It wasn't. A "citadel city" was usually built on a road to a major city (like Pergamum). The only reason it was there was to slow down an approaching army. Its only purpose was to basically forewarn the larger city that an opposing army was on its way, and then it was to become "cannon fodder" in order to protect the larger city.

Even though Thyatira wasn't very large, it did have a busy commercial center. It was on a major road of the Roman Empire, and, because of this, many trade unions had settled in this city. Everyone who worked in Thyatira had to be a member of one of the trade unions. There were carpenters, dyers, sellers of goods, tent makers, etc.

The Apostle Paul and Silas might have visited Thyatira during Paul's second or third journey, although the evidence is entirely circumstantial. They visited several small, unnamed towns in the general vicinity during their second journey. While in Philippi, Paul and Silas stayed with a woman named Lydia from Thyatira, who continued to help them even after they were jailed and released. Lydia was a "dealer in purple cloth" and a "worshiper of God." (Acts 16:14-15)

The reference to Lydia suggests the city's significance in connection with the dye industry, and perhaps also the relative freedom and mobility of at least some of its women in pursuing careers. The purple dye that was made and sold in Thyatira was world famous. It basically came from two sources. One source was a root called the Madder-root which grew around Thyatira. The other was a little tropical sea snail called Murex. From the mucus of that tiny little sea creature came one drop of precious purple dye. Because it was very difficult to get the dye out of the Madder-root and even more difficult to get it out of the Murex, it was very costly. So this little city flourished as a commercial center for purple dye and for the garments that would go along with the industry. Actually, Thyatira, which is now the modern city Akhisar is still famous today for its dyes.

Among the ruins, inscriptions have been found relating to the guild of dyers in that city in ancient times. These trade guilds, were more organized in Thyatira than in any other ancient city. These guilds wielded great influence in the city. What I found interesting is that each guild had a different god or deity they worshipped. So basically, if you associated yourself with a guild, you were in essence part of a religious group.

Pagan feasts, were often associated with these guilds. It was taught by the early church that no Christian could belong to any of the guilds. So these trade guilds presented themselves as opposition to Christianity. In order to have good standing in the guild you would need to participate in the guild activities. If you did not engage yourself in the guild activities, you could easily be out of a job. So let's say you are a Christian working in the trades in Thyatira. The guild had routine activities, which often involved sacrifices and feasts to a certain deity. Sometimes these feasts could include certain immoral activities. As a part of this guild, you would be expected to participate in the activities and worship the guild god. What do you do? If you don't participate in the activities you could lose your job.

I want you to understand the sense of what was involved here in Thyatira and the pressure the followers of Jesus were under.

The principal deity of the city was Apollo (He was the son of Zeus and had a twin sister Artemis); and there were several lesser deities that were worshipped here.

The letter to this church was written sometime towards the end of the first century. By the end of the second century the church in Thyatira did not exist. It wasn't from persecution. It wasn't pressure from the guilds or their false gods and pagan ways. The church had fallen from within. Much like what is happening in the church today. We are not failing because of the atheists . . . it is not the cults or even the liberal agenda. The church in America is falling from within. As I mentioned in the last chapter, pornography is one of the greatest threats to the church today. Another great threat to the church would be the lack of belief in absolute truth. A majority of Christians today feel that truth is relative. What is relative truth? Basically if something is true for me, it may not be true for you. For example the Bible teaches that sex outside of marriage is a sin. To the next person, having sex before marriage is not a sin. It is relative because our culture says that sex before marriage is OK. A report in the Los Angeles Times quoted George Barna as determining that:

- Only 44 percent of evangelicals are certain that absolute moral truth exists.

- Only nine percent of evangelical teens believe in absolute moral truth. [51]

The apologist, writer Josh McDowell, paints an even a bleaker picture of the lack of absolute moral truth among Christians.

According to Josh McDowell, in 1990 about 51 percent of evangelical Christians did not believe in absolute truth. By 1994 the percentage escalated to 62 percent. In 1999, it jumped to 78 percent. Want to guess what it is today? According to Josh McDowell, *"It is one of the most staggering statistics in history of the church. 91percent of evangelical Christians said there is no absolute truth."* [52]

Personally I think those numbers may be a little high, but regardless there are a lot of Christians who are off base spiritually.

What a tragedy for evangelicals to declare proudly that a personal conversion and new birth in Christ are at the center of their faith and then to defy biblical moral standards by living almost as sinfully as their pagan neighbors. This letter to the church in Thyatira is the longest of the seven letters. It may have been the lengthiest letter because Thyatira was the most corrupt of the churches.

This letter follows closely to the letter to Pergamum. How? What was beginning to happen in Pergamos had come to full bloom in Thyatira. Let's take a look at this letter.

18 *"Write this letter to the angel of the church in Thyatira. This is the message from the Son of God, whose eyes are like flames of fire, whose feet are like polished bronze:* 19 *I know all the things you do. I have seen your love, your faith, your service, and your patient endurance. And I can see your constant improvement in all these things.*

20 *But I have this complaint against you. You are permitting that woman—that Jezebel who calls herself a prophet—to lead my servants astray. She teaches them to commit sexual sin and to eat food offered to idols.* 21 *I gave her time to repent, but she does not want to turn away from her immorality.*

22 *Therefore, I will throw her on a bed of suffering, and those who commit adultery with her will suffer greatly unless they repent and turn away from her evil deeds.* 23 *I will strike her children dead. Then all the churches will know that I am the one who searches out the thoughts and intentions of every person. And I will give to each of you whatever you deserve.*

24 *But I also have a message for the rest of you in Thyatira who have not followed this false teaching ('deeper truths,' as they call them—depths of Satan, actually). I will ask nothing more of you* 25 *except that you hold tightly to what you have until I come.* 26 *To all who are victorious, who obey me to the very end; to them I will give authority*

over all the nations. 27 They will rule the nations with an iron rod and smash them like clay pots. 28 They will have the same authority I received from my Father, and I will also give them the morning star! 29 Anyone with ears to hear must listen to the Spirit and understand what he is saying to the churches." See . . . I told you it was long!

I want you to notice first of all that Jesus identifies Himself as the Son of God. That is His messianic title. That means that He is deity. He is one with God in essence. He is the Son of God. I know some people who claim that Jesus never said that he was the Son of God. I'm not sure how they come up with that. Here is one of several places in the New Testament where He makes that claim very clearly.

In Chapter 1 of Revelation, verse 13, John describes Jesus as the Son of Man. Whenever He is designated Son of Man it is emphasizing His humanness. That makes Jesus sympathetic to what is going on in our lives. He understands us because He knows what it is like to be a human. He understands the trials of His church, the needs of His church and the temptations of His church.

By verse 18 in chapter 2, John is not emphasizing Jesus in His humility; He's emphasizing Him in His divine power. He's emphasizing Jesus' deity. The party is over; there is no more sympathy. When it comes to this particular church and what is going on, Jesus is coming as the judge. He is coming as the God who does not tolerate sin.

This "Son of God" you will notice has *"eyes like flames of fire and feet like polished bronze."* This means that Jesus has piercing vision. He sees everything and nothing is hidden from him. You can't cover it up, you can't disguise it ... Jesus sees everything for what it is. His fiery eyes are mentioned in several other verses in Scripture:

- Revelation 19:12 -*"His eyes were like flames of fire."*

- Daniel 10:6 -*"His face flashed like lightning, and his eyes flamed like torches."*

These are the eyes of the Son of God. He pierces every facade. He sees into the remotest recesses. He sees the hidden things of the soul and of the church. This church may have had a good reputation on the outside. It may even have had something of notoriety among other churches. But the Son of God's penetrating eyes uncover everything. He is able to see into the secret places of their hearts.

Next, the text says that He has feet *"like polished bronze"* which can trample sin under foot and severely punish that which is wrong.

This is how Jesus introduces Himself to the church in Thyatira. He is going to come to them in judgment. Frankly, it is a terrifying picture. Can you imagine what happened in the church at Thyatira when the letter was delivered and read? Can you imagine this happening to a local church today? You get a letter from Jesus saying that the church you attend is in disfavor with the Lord and will be judged if found guilty. I can see some of the congregation jumping ship and the next Sunday attending a church in a different city.

Hebrews 10:27 tells us that God will come in judgment with the fury of a fire, which will consume His adversaries. If something doesn't change in Thyatira, they're going to be caught in severe judgment. Jesus Christ needs to be taken seriously because He is the Holy and Righteous Judge. He is not your "brother or friend" or "the man upstairs." He is the Son of God and our coming Judge.

Let's look at verse 19: "*I know all the things you do. I have seen your love, your faith, your service, and your patient endurance. And I can see your constant improvement in all these things.*"

Now, there were some good things going on in this church. Jesus tells us what they are. He says I *have seen your **love**, your **faith**, your **service** and your **patient endurance**.* Jesus says they are actually improving in all

146

these things. If we had been living in Thyatira in the first century, we would have seen a thriving community. This body of believers would have probably impressed us. It must have seemed very attractive, at least on the outside.

Here is an interesting fact: of the seven churches, Thyatira is the only body of believers singled out for their love.

Jesus tells them you are really doing some great things . . . but! I can see the believers in Thyatira hearing these words, looking at each other, smiling and nodding their heads in agreement. It was good news; they were doing great . . . but!

Here it comes. In verse 20 Jesus says, *"But I have this complaint against you. You are permitting that woman—that Jezebel who calls herself a prophet—to lead my servants astray. She teaches them to commit sexual sin and to eat food offered to idols."*

Jesus begins His scathing rebuke with those familiar words. Do you remember Jesus speaking these very same words to the church in Ephesus (cf. Revelation 2:4). Ephesus was strong in doctrine but weak in love. Thyatira was strong in love but weak in doctrine. Evidently there was in this church at Thyatira a woman who was a very dominant leader. Jesus names her "Jezebel." Now that was not her name, of course, but our Lord always names people according to their character. Here he chooses the name of the most evil woman in the Old Testament. If you are not familiar with the name of Jezebel, here is the "*Readers Digest* version."

The Old Testament Jezebel was the daughter of the King of Sidon, a town in what is now Lebanon. She was the wife of King Ahab of Israel, which was in the Northern Kingdom. She is particularly noted for having made the worship of the god Baal popular in Israel. Queen Jezebel led King Ahab away from worshipping God to serve this false god, Baal. Baal was a fertility god, and his worship involved immoral and licentious practices.

Through intimidation, deception and just plain conniving, she got Ahab to propagate her idolatrous teaching throughout Israel. It was Jezebel who spread Baal worship widely among the 10 tribes of Israel until it became one of the more popular religions of the day. She herself supported over 800 prophets of Baal, who ate at her table. She was the one who tried to kill Elijah after his famous encounter with 480 of the prophets of Baal on Mt. Carmel. She was also the one who murdered her neighbor Naboth because her husband wanted his vineyard.

She was a ruthless, immoral, and a seducer of people, and that is why Jesus selects her name for this dominant woman at Thyatira. But like all evil people, she gets it in the end. My favorite part of this story is when Jezebel justly meets her end by being thrown from her palace window into the courtyard below where the dogs came and gnawed at her body and licked up her blood. Good Old Testament stuff.

Jesus' initial charge to these believers is that they permitted—or better yet tolerated—the teachings of this Jezebel. Notice his anger is toward them and not Jezebel. Jesus was angry at these believers for tolerating false teaching and sinful behavior rather than confronting and condemning it.

The Jezebel in the Old Testament led the people of Israel to commit sexual sin and worship idols. And this woman is identified as Jezebel because she did the same thing in the church. At the end of verse 20, it says that she led the bondservants of Christ to commit acts of immorality and eat things sacrificed to idols.

This Jezebel in Thyatira called herself a "prophetess." Let me just say that there is nothing wrong with that in itself. I want to make clear that it was not her being female that was wrong—it was the content of her teaching. There have been other women prophets in the Bible. The Old Testament lists a number of them who were well respected in Israel.

In the book of Acts, we are told that the evangelist Philip had four daughters who were prophetesses and had prophesied within the church. The trouble with Jezebel is that she was a *false* prophetess. Jesus clearly points out what was wrong with her teachings. She taught that it was all right for Christians to indulge in sexual immorality and idolatry.

We need to revisit these trade unions or guilds in Thyatira. Remember earlier in this chapter, I mentioned that in order to work in these guilds, you were required to worship their deity, follow their rules and pagan practices? Scottish Scholar William Barclay writes about these trades: *"These guilds met frequently, and they met for a common meal. Such a meal was, at least in part, a religious ceremony. It would probably meet in a heathen temple, and it would certainly begin with a libation to the gods, and the meal itself would largely consist of meat offered to idols. The official position of the church meant that a Christian could not attend such a meal."*[53]

This was the problem the believers in Thyatira faced. In order to make a living they had to belong to a guild, but to attend the guild was to become involved, or to be pressured to become involved, with the worship of idols and with immorality. So they had to make a choice.

Apparently Jezebel had begun to teach that it was all right for them to go along with the requirements of the guild, that they needed to submit to the pressures of the world around them in order to make a living, and that God would understand and overlook this. Verse 20 says that she was literally teaching and misleading servants of God to commit sexual immorality and to eat things sacrificed to idols.

I can hardly imagine worship and open sexual perversion together. Generally speaking, in our society nearly all religions make at least a pretense of teaching the values of marriage, family and faithfulness. But that is changing.

Let me ask you, what things do we worship other than God. What "things" do we hold onto? What about our love of money, our jobs or our possessions? How about the things we watch? What sins do we tolerate? Notice that the Lord holds the church responsible. His accusation to them is, "You tolerate that woman Jezebel."

This is a serious problem that church leadership has to face in our day just as it had to face it in the first century.

Notice that in the letters to the church at Pergamum, and to the church at Thyatira, the Lord links sexual immorality with idolatry. If we stop to think about it, one inevitably leads to the other. The reason is this: fornication and adultery are both clear-cut violations of specific and explicit statements in the Word of God. Anyone who reads the Bible can see very clearly that God forbids these activities. It is wrong for believers to indulge in sexual immorality of any sort. When one does, he or she has deliberately violated the authority of God.

Jesus wants us to understand that this woman is causing true believers to be led astray and the church is tolerating it. The church is sitting by passively and allowing this to happen. That is what was going on in Thyatira.

On the other hand, God is such a gracious God. Notice the grace in Jesus words in verse 21. *"I gave her time to repent, but she does not want to turn away from her immorality."*

Is that not gracious? He gave her time to repent, but she did not want to turn away from her sin. God always gives an opportunity for repentance. Notice that Jesus says, "She was unwilling." And so the judgment must come. The impact of that judgment is given in verse 22-23: 22 *"Therefore, I will throw her on a bed of suffering, and those who commit adultery with her will suffer greatly unless they repent and turn away from her evil deeds. 23 I will strike her children dead. Then all the churches will know that I am the one who searches out the thoughts and intentions of every person. And I will give to each of you whatever you deserve."*

Notice that here are actually three parties involved in this coming judgment.

First, there is Jezebel herself. Jesus says, "(Because of her unrepentant heart) I *will throw her on a bed of suffering.*" I sense a little sarcasm here. What exactly could this bed be? It could be sickness or even death. We don't really know.

My mom used to always say to me whenever I got into trouble, "*You've made your bed, now you can lie in it.*"

Whatever the judgment is that Jesus is declaring for this woman, it will cause much pain and suffering.

Then there is a second group: "*those who commit adultery with her will suffer greatly* (literally, "I will give them great affliction") *unless they repent and turn away from her evil deeds.*" Those who were participants in these pagan actions of immorality and idolatry will suffer the consequences. The suffering and "great affliction" that he refers to in this verse could very possibly be sexual disease. Just for your information, gonorrhea and syphilis were well known diseases and widespread throughout the ancient world.

As for the third group, the Lord says, "*I will strike her children with death.*" I believe these children represent her followers. I don't think He means the believers who were following her. I think this refers to the others who were involved in this practice. I think this teaching had been around for a long time in the church. Remember, we're in 96 AD and this church has been around for possibly 40 years. This has been going on long enough that there is a second generation of people propagating the same stuff. Those are her children. She has begotten a generation of followers who are advocating the same thing.

The "death" in this verse I believe, refers to spiritual death, in what is called "the second death." This second death is destruction in the lake of fire is described in Chapters 20 and 21 of this book. It is a commitment to evil that makes repentance difficult.

Look at the last part of verse 23: " . . . *Then all the churches will know that I am the one who searches out the thoughts and intentions of every person. And I will give to each of you whatever you deserve."*

Jesus is saying, "I want my church pure. Your church isn't pure. You have a woman named Jezebel who is leading my people astray. I am going to punish her. And then those of you who are my followers, who have been involved in this immorality and idolatry, if you do not repent immediately, I am going to punish you severely and it may even cost some of you your lives."

Remember what happened to Ananias and Sapphira when they sinned against the Lord? (Acts 5:1-11) God is not to be mocked. I hope you get the picture that Christ wants His church pure.

Discipline in the church has two purposes: one is correction and repentance in the sinning person's life. Another purpose is restoration—always the goal of biblical discipline is to bring the person back to the Lord. But discipline also has the purpose of instilling a healthy respect for the Lord in the people of God. Jezebel had time to repent and didn't do it. He cries out to those who have followed her to repent while they have time. And that's the message He wants the church to hear.

If you're involved in sin, you must repent; you're not only in danger of chastening, but if you continue on in sin you could even be in danger of death.

And then the warning is broadened at the end of verse 23: "*And I will give to each of you what you deserve.*"

And now He's talking to every believer in the church. What does Jesus mean by this "each of us will get what we deserve?" You might be thinking "so where does forgiveness come into all of this?" Don't the scriptures teach us that: "*He has cast our sins behind his back . . . God will not count our sins against . . . He will separate our sins as far as the East is from the West . . . and He will bury them in the deepest sea?*" (2 Corinthians 5:19; Psalm 103:12; Micah 7:19; Isaiah 38:17)

Of course the Scriptures teach us that there is forgiveness for believers who repent of their sin. But then we read passages like the last part of verse 23, which, indicates that we will be held accountable for our deeds. So, the question comes up: *Are you saying that I am going to be judged by what I do? Are you saying I am going to be judged by my works?*

Yep . . . and it is biblical.

Look at Romans 2:6-7a: 6 *"He will judge everyone according to what they have done. 7 He will give eternal life to those who keep on doing good . . ."*

How about Alexander the coppersmith who did the Apostle Paul much harm? Paul says that the Lord will repay him (what) *"according to his deeds."* (2 Timothy 4:14) That is, and always has been, and always will be the divine principle for judgment.

Matthew 7 tells us, *"We will know them by their fruit."* Again, the deeds are the issue. Another passage in Matthew 16 tells us: 27 *"For the Son of Man will come with his angels in the glory of his Father and will judge all people according to their deeds."*

One more verse: *"Look, I am coming soon, bringing my reward with me to repay all people according to their deeds."* Revelation 22:12

Does it sound like God is concerned about the things we do? Of course He is. Now we as Christians may not lose out on heaven because of our deeds, but it could cost us crowns and reward.

Honestly, we don't know what happened to the Jezebel in the church in Tyratira? Did God kill off Jezebel? Did God judge and punish those who followed her? We don't know. The Scriptures and early church writings don't tell us. We do know that within the next 100 years the church in Thyatira ceased to exist.

Let me emphasize again that I am not saying that works saves you. Your deeds demonstrate your spiritual condition. God can look at us and see that we are his. As Christians, we can let others know that we are believers because of the fruit of the Spirit that we manifest in our lives.

If you truly belong to God there will be fruit; it may be small and hard to see, but it's there. If you call yourself a Christian and there is no fruit in your life, then it's a good chance you are not who you call yourself.

What fruit am I talking about? The fruit of the Spirit found in Galatians 5:22: *"But the Holy Spirit produces this kind of fruit in our lives: love, joy, peace, patience, kindness, goodness, faithfulness, gentleness, and self-control."*

You may be thinking, *"Those believers in Thyatira lived a long, long time ago. So what does this passage have to do with our church today? In our church today we don't take a casual corporate attitude toward sexual immorality, and we certainly don't promote idolatry."*

I hope that is true for your church. But I don't want you to be congratulating yourselves too soon. One of the things you discover readily when you read the Old Testament is that adultery and fornication are often used as symbols of spiritual unfaithfulness. Israel is often accused of adultery even when no sexual immorality is involved.

When God's people put other things ahead of Him—whether it be success, prosperity, materialism, sports, fitness, financial security, or even ministry—He becomes jealous because we are being unfaithful to Him. God will tolerate no other lovers. The seductive teaching of Jezebel is a real danger in our churches today.

Every generation of believers must face the question, *"How far should I go in accepting and adopting the cultural standards and behaviors of my day?"* Where does being contemporary cross over into compromise? The problem is that we Christians are caught between two worlds—citizens of two countries—and we cannot renounce either. We are citizens of earth and at the same time citizens of heaven.

As I stated in an earlier chapter, the statistics tell us that today there is little if any observable difference between people who call themselves Christian and those who don't. Let me ask? What about you? Could the same be said of you? Are you any different from those outside the church? In what ways have you compromised your faith? We each need to take a good look at ourselves. Remember, each of us will be judged according to our deeds.

Let's get back to Revelation 2. So there were those within the congregation who were concerned they might be swept up with the coming judgment. He answers them in verse 24: *"But I also have a message for the rest of you in Thyatira who have not followed this false teaching ('deeper truths,' as they call them—depths of Satan, actually). I will ask nothing more of you 25 except that you hold tightly to what you have until I come."*

Those had to be encouraging words for those who were not involved in this false teaching. Jesus says I ask nothing more of you than to just hang in there until I return. And then Jesus gives some words of counsel: 26 *"To all who are victorious, who obey me to the very end, to them I will give authority over all the nations. 27 They will rule the nations with an iron rod and smash them like clay pots. 28 They will have the same authority I received from my Father, and I will also give them the morning star!"*

Who are the ones who are victorious in this verse? The true believers. John 14:15 says, *"If you love me, obey my commandments."* If you truly love God, you will be obedient.

First John 2 makes it very clear: 3 *"And we can be sure that we know him if we obey his commandments. 4 If someone claims, 'I know God,' but doesn't obey God's commandments, that person is a liar and is not living in the truth. 5 But those who obey God's word truly show how completely they love him. That is how we know we are living in him. 6 Those who say they live in God should live their lives as Jesus did."* 1 John 2:3-6

Can it get any clearer than that? Notice in verse 26, Jesus gives the clearest definition of an overcomer in these seven letters: *"he who keeps My deeds until the end."* Jesus tells us that someday we will rule the nations. What a glorious promise. Verse 27 is a quotation from Psalm 2:9 *"They will rule the nations with an iron rod and smash them like clay pots"*

It is a reference to the rule of Christ in the earthly kingdom that we dispensationalist's[54] like to call "The Millennium." If you do not believe in a physical reign on earth by Jesus Christ (Amillennialism), you can go ahead and skip to the next chapter.

The reward for our faithfulness will be the privilege of reigning with Christ in His earthly kingdom. Believers who are faithful will receive authority in heaven from Jesus Christ and will "rule" (literally shepherd) others during Christ's 1000 year reign on earth.

Where you sit and rule will depend on how you live now. You may not live in a position of power now, but if you serve the Lord faithfully, God will give you a position of power and prestige in His kingdom. Do you think this is worthy of working for? I think so.

Notice the Psalmist tells us, *"They will rule the nations with an iron rod and smash them like clay pots."*

You might be asking after reading verse 27, "What's with all this rod stuff? Who gets hit with the rod of iron during the millennial kingdom?" Remember it is referring not to the new heaven and the new earth (because nothing evil ever enters there), but to the millennial kingdom, the earthly kingdom over which the saints will share a reign with Christ. Jesus says you are going to participate and rule in His Kingdom. We will be there to see the nations of the world, forced to bow the knee to Jesus Christ as He rules as the King of kings and Lord and lords. Every person, every king, every ruler, every nation that continues to refuse Him and bow before Him as Lord will be dashed, broken and crushed as fragile pottery. He will bring thrones and rulers down to nothing and bring wrath upon those that "refused to love the truth and so be saved."

What a great promise to those who are victorious.

So what is this "morning star" we are to receive? In Revelation 22:16, Jesus says of himself: " . . . *I am the bright and morning star.*" Jesus also says that He will give the overcomer the "morning star." Jesus is promising all overcomers His own eternal presence for Jesus is the bright morning star. I believe that believers will experience great intimacy with their Lord.

Peter wrote in 2 Peter 1:19 that if we are Christians, the morning star has already dawned in our hearts. And some day in the future we'll have Him in His fullness. But there also seems to be another emphasis. The text literally says, "the star, the morning one."

This means the brilliant or bright one, the brightest of all the stars. The star of the morning may be considered the brightest, and the symbolism here indicates the glory that the righteous will experience in the coming kingdom. Daniel the prophet says it best: "*Those who are wise will shine as bright as the sky, and those who lead many to righteousness will shine like the stars forever.*" Daniel 12:3

Jesus closes this letter with the familiar call: "*He who has an ear, let him hear what the Spirit says to the churches.*"

All seven letters close with this statement. Yet, beginning with this letter, the last four letters place this call after the promises to the overcomer. Again, we see the personal and loving concern of the Spirit of God for His people and His desire that we all respond in faith and obedience.

These words are not just to this church, but to all the churches. These promises and warnings are needed in our individual lives, no matter what our local church may be like.

These are tremendously practical letters for the age in which we live. We need to heed them today as much as they did in the first century. So what have I have learned from this? Several things stand out.

One, God takes sin in the church very seriously. Believers needs to practice true repentance, understand the fullness of God's grace in their lives and live out their true identity in Christ as well as allowing the power of the Holy Spirit to control their life.

The second thing that stands out in this passage is "accountability." Not only is the church going to be held accountable for its actions, but also each of us is going to be judged according to our deeds. We will each stand "mano-a-mano" before the Lord Jesus Christ. We will be held accountable for all our thoughts, all our words and all our deeds. This will not be a judgment of salvation but for rewards. It will be evidence of walking a true Christian life.

The third thing I see here is the wonderful and gracious promise of God to His children. We have been promised that if we are faithful and obedient we will rule with Christ Jesus in His Kingdom.

What a promise!

Questions for Thoughtful Discussion

1. What or who do you worship? What do you hold on to that keeps you from being fully devoted to God? What is stopping you from following God?

2. Are you any different from the unsaved people who are around you at work, or at school? Does the culture of this country affect the way you live for God?

3. Define moral truth. Do you believe in the absolute truth of the scripture? Does it affect the way you live or do you pick and choose what you believe?

4. Do you believe that God is concerned about our actions? Does your life daily demonstrate the fruit of the Spirit? Why not? Would others see Christ through how you live your life?

Chapter 6

THE CHURCH AT SARDIS — *D.O.A.*

I n 1960, my parents packed up the family 1955 Chevy with all of our belongings and headed west from the dreariness of Pittsburgh, PA to the sunshine of Phoenix, Arizona. Back then Phoenix was a sleepy little town of just under 500,000 residents. We had a few celebrities who grew up in the Phoenix area. Film director Steven Spielberg and actress Linda Carter both attended Arcadia High School. We had the musicians Alice Cooper and Wayne Newton. Famous news anchors Hugh Downs and Paul Harvey were long time residents.

Over the years a lot of famous people moved into the "Valley of the Sun" and called it home. Folks like Muhammad Ali, Danica Patrick, Stevie Nicks, Glenn Campbell, Bret Michaels and George Takei just to name a few.

Why is this important . . . it's not. My point is that if all these famous people lived in one city in the first century, they would have probably lived in the tiny town of Sardis. Sardis was considered one of the most beautiful cities in the world. Sardis would have been the place where the ancient celebrities lived and played.

Alexander the Great kept a home there even after he built the city of Smyrna. Cyrus the Great lived in Sardis for a while. Antiochus the Great had a home in Sardis. Anybody who was anybody in the ancient world probably had a home in Sardis.

So let's take a look at this city.

Sardis was the ancient capital of Lydia. Because of the inaccessible plateau where the city was originally built, it was an ideal military fortress. The acropolis of Sardis rose straight up about 1,500 ft. and had only one narrow, winding, steep road of entry. It was an impregnable fortress. Rather, it *should* have been, but the Sardian military was...well...somewhat incompetent.

Worried about the growing power of the Persians, the Lydian ruler Croesus offered lavish gifts in the Temple of Apollo at Delphi where the oracle told him that if he made war on the Persian ruler, Cyrus the Great, "a great empire would be destroyed." Based on the information the oracle offered, he attacked Cyrus but was forced to retreat to Sardis where he suffered a siege. Somewhere around 547 BC., Cyrus conquered Sardis. Ancient historian Herodotus recorded the shock of the Lydian defeat, as the city was considered impregnable. It seems the oracle was correct, but the "destroyed" kingdom was that of Croesus, not Cyrus.

Cyrus spared Croesus' life and made him his advisor, and Sardis became the headquarters for Persian administration in western Asia Minor. Another side note about Cyrus: Cyrus the Great was the one who defeated Babylon, threw Daniel into the lion's den and eventually allowed the Jews to return to Jerusalem.

Remember that I said the army of Sardis was incompetent? The rock on which Sardis was built is friable, which means that while the slopes were steep, because of the cracks and faults, it was climbable. During the siege, one of Cyrus' soldiers had noticed a Sardian soldier climbing down this slope to retrieve a helmet he had dropped. Cyrus concluded that the slopes were negotiable in that particular spot so that night a raiding party of Persian troops climbed quite easily up to the citadel by following the fault line. When they reached the battlements they found them unguarded, for the Sardian's considered them too safe to need a guard. It is said that even a child could have defended the city from this kind of an attack by watching that one area where the wall could have been scaled, but not so much as one observer had been appointed to watch that side because it was believed to be inaccessible, and so the city was conquered. Kind of reminds me of Babylon and how the Persians entered the city.

Sardis remained under Persian domination until it surrendered to Alexander the Great in 334 BC. As Alexander the Great approached the city, the leaders of Sardis ran out to surrender the city before Alexander could join battle. As you can see fighting wasn't one of their strengths.

Sardis was the world center for the international jewelry trade. The nearby mountains were dotted with gold mines thus making the city the monetary capital of the region.

There was actually a river that flowed into the center of the city. The riverbed was said to be lined with gold. Why? Because the slag from the mines eventually flowed into the river.

It was during the reign of King Croesus that the metallurgists of Sardis discovered the secret of separating gold from silver, thereby producing both metals of a purity never known before.

Their jewelry was renown throughout the empire. In 1968 an archeological dig discovered a gold refinery that was located in the city.

Being situated in a mountainous region, the city was earthquake-prone. Sardis, like neighboring Philadelphia, suffered a catastrophic earthquake in AD 17. This caused the sudden collapse of the plateau where the city stood.

Because of the earthquakes, the people eventually abandoned the collapsed and destroyed city. They soon discovered how fertile the soil in the surrounding valley was so many of the people turned to farming as a means of livelihood, specifically to the cultivation of vineyards.

There seemed to be a large Jewish contingent living in Sardis. The synagogue in Sardis was one of the most impressive ancient synagogues yet discovered outside Palestine. As I mentioned earlier, the origins of the Jewish community at Sardis started when the Seleucid King Antiochus III encouraged Jews from Babylonia and other countries to settle in the city. [55]

Connected to the synagogue was a large bathhouse/gymnasium. Several of the rooms in the synagogue were used as changing rooms. The Sardis synagogue provides evidence for the continued growth of Jewish communities in Asia Minor, their integration into general Roman imperial civic life, and their size and importance at a time when many scholars previously assumed that Christianity had eclipsed Judaism. Not only was there a Jewish synagogue, but Sardis also worshipped its fair share of deities. The patron deity was named Cybele and was believed to possess the power and ability of restoring the dead back to life. The Romans built a temple for their goddess Artemis and a large bath-gymnasium complex. Yes, it is the same bathhouse that was connected to the synagogue.

It is believed that the Apostle John founded the church in Sardis. Others think the Apostle Paul may have started the church, and another line of thinking is it was started by one of his disciples. In other words, we don't have the foggiest idea who planted the church in Sardis. But the church did exist in Sardis.

The Caesar-cult also existed in Sardis and had become quite popular around 17 AD. There is no direct reference made to this problem in this letter, and neither is there any evidence of persecution. Not only did the Jewish synagogue have the Temple of Cybele adjoining it, but also there is archaeological evidence that the temple to Artemis was adjacent to a home where believers met and worshipped. Many inscriptions of crosses have been found in and around the temple of Artemis, indicating that it may have been partly transformed into a Christian place of worship.

Let's take a look at the letter to the believers in Sardis.

"Write this letter to the angel of the church in Sardis. This is the message from the one who has the sevenfold Spirit of God and the seven stars . . . "

In this letter Jesus describes Himself as the One who "has the sevenfold Spirit of God and the seven stars." The word "has" (echon) conveys both ownership and control. Jesus holds or possesses the seven spirits and stars.

The number "seven" is the number for perfection or fullness. These symbols are identified for us in the first chapter of Revelation. The "seven spirits" are a symbol of the Holy Spirit in his fullness. This does not mean that there are seven Holy Spirits. There is only one Spirit of God. What this church at Sardis desperately needed was the Spirit of God. I think that is one of the issues with many churches today. They need the Spirit of God in their lives.

In my opinion and experience . . . a lot of churches set up their ministries and run their church programs according to the latest business standards than by dependence on the Holy Spirit. For example, when I was pastoring a small church in Oregon, my email and church mail were inundated with advertisements and magazines promising to help me grow my church.

Articles such as *"5 Barriers to Church Growth,"* or *"10 Do's and Don'ts of Growing a Healthy Church."* My favorite was something about *"How to Increase Your Church's Giving Units."*

Where is the Holy Spirit in this? If your church is run by "human power" you could find yourself in the same condition as the church in Sardis . . . dead in the water.

The "seven stars" refer to the seven messengers, shepherds, pastors, elders, or leaders of the seven churches. Take your pick . . . choose your favorite!

The next few verses go right for the jugular.

" . . . *I know all the things you do, and that you have a reputation for being alive—but you are dead. 2 Wake up! Strengthen what little remains, for even what is left is almost dead. I find that your actions do not meet the requirements of my God. 3 Go back to what you heard and believed at first; hold to it firmly. Repent and turn to me again. If you don't wake up, I will come to you suddenly, as unexpected as a thief.*"

Jesus declares, "I know all the things you do . . . I know your deeds." That which is invisible to us is perfectly clear to the Lord who is in the business of revealing our true condition regardless of how spiritual we may think we are.

Jesus knows everything, absolutely everything. Notice that He doesn't commend this church.

Why?

Because there isn't anything to commend them for.

With each of the previous four churches, Jesus begins with uplifting words of commendation. But when Jesus speaks to the church in Sardis, He starts with a word of condemnation.

He does so because a dead church is deadly to the cause of Christ. Matthew 5:13 *"You are the salt of the earth. But what good is salt if it has lost its flavor? Can you make it salty again? It will be thrown out and trampled underfoot as worthless."*

Let me ask you a question. Is your church dead? Your first response would probably be, "No way!" How would you know? What would Jesus be saying about your church?

The fact is there are dead churches out there. They may have the greatest programs; they may have a very popular preacher who gives great sermons; they could even have great worship and give to missions. But they very well could be dead. The problem is we look at our churches through our eyes and we think everything looks great but Jesus sees it all. We may think we have our act together and Jesus is saying: "Your church looks alive, but it is dead."

You may be saying "Chris you are crazy. How can a church be dead? Isn't that some kind of oxymoron?"

How can you have a dead church? How can a congregation be dead if the living Lord indwells it? You would think this would be impossible. But sadly, it's not.

There are some commentators out there that say the church of Sardis was full of unredeemed and unregenerate people. In other words they were mostly unsaved. I don't believe that to be true. Some could have been only professing believers, but you need to remember that unlike churches today, not everyone would be invited to join a congregation. Many of the churches would be underground and very cautious about who they let get involved. But I don't think that is the emphasis here. Jesus was talking to true believers who were spiritually carnal and working from the energy of their own resources. This church just was looking good on the outside, but they weren't making a dent in the eternal. This is a warning. A church is in danger of death. How?

- When it begins to worship its own past or history, its reputation or name, or the "celebrities" who attend their services

- When it is more concerned with form over function and programs are more important than people.

- When it is more concerned with numbers and "giving units," than with the spiritual quality of life it should be producing in its people.

We have mega churches that have been styled as *"cathedrals of consumption"*[56] because they are designed to feed our consumer appetites. If we want it, they have it—coffee shops, bookstores, bowling alleys, fitness centers, climbing walls and even alcohol-free nightclubs—if it attracts people, they will have it, all under the pretense of "evangelizing the masses."

It is important to recognize that the church in Sardis doesn't appear dead. This church has a reputation for being alive. People are impressed. This church's deadness is not man's evaluation but God's.

Whenever you read about deadness in the spiritual dimension in the New Testament, it is always connected with one thing. It is always connected with sin.

Ephesians 2:1 says, *"Once you were dead because of your disobedience and your many sins."*

Deadness is the result of sin. Colossians chapter 2 and verse 13, *"You were dead because of your sins and because your sinful nature . . . "*

That is why Jesus tells them:

2 *"Wake up! Strengthen what little remains, for even what is left is almost dead. I find that your actions do not meet the requirements of my God."*

- The first need of a church that is dying or dead is to awaken to its condition.

- These words in Greek are staccato commands, sharp words, like a slap in the face, designed to stimulate, to wake up.

The term "wake up" conveys the notion that God's people can be spiritually asleep when they should be awake. Jesus uses a very effective metaphor. In the physical realm, when we are asleep we are unconcerned, apathetic and indifferent. Unfortunately, the same can be true in the spiritual realm. Many Christians have dozed off and they don't even know it. They are in need of an abrupt wake-up call. The Greek word translated "wake up" can also be translated "keep being watchful." Jesus wants His church to be vigilant. The word "strengthen" means "to establish or stabilize something."

This is likely a reference to various opportunities remaining for this church. Sardis is living on borrowed time. I truly believe that no matter how "screwed up" a church may be, God still has a purpose for it, if it repents and secures a right relationship with the Lord.

What about the second part of this verse?

What does He mean by "*I find that your actions do not meet the requirements of my God*? I believe Jesus was saying that their works were incomplete and unfinished. Their actions were right, but their motives were wrong. They were not doing them for the right reason.

As you read this you can see that here is a church that is busy doing good things, but doing them to impress people. They were trying to display and enhance a reputation they had. I think they were concerned as to whether people around would see, and know what they were doing. But notice Jesus says that even those good deeds were about to die. "Strengthen them," he says.

How? By putting their motives right!

All through the Scriptures we are told God judges not the things we do, but the reason we do them. He reads our hearts. He is judging whether our work is done out of love for Him and gratitude for what He has done for us and is unconcerned whether people see them or not.

I have a friend who was a pastor of a large church and had a very successful ministry.

Years after he left that ministry, he confided to me that most of the success of the church wasn't really the Lord's doing but his. As we walked along a local beach in California he confessed that the success of his church was pretty much man-made. He said, "*You really don't need the*

Holy Spirit to have a successful church. I never really gave the Spirit of God a second thought as I was building my ministry." Talk about honesty. It makes me wonder how many "successful" churches out there are man-made?

I know I struggled with this issue when I was pastoring. It was always easier to do things "my way" than it was to seek the direction from the Spirit. Besides, how was I to discern His direction from my direction? Was I doing things God's way or my way? I just always assumed that my direction would be His direction. I was trying to grow His church. That is something pastors need to think about. Whose church are they really building?

Jesus goes on to tell them,

3 *"Go back to what you heard and believed at first; hold to it firmly. Repent and turn to me again. If you don't wake up, I will come to you suddenly, as unexpected as a thief."*

Verse 3 in the Greek literally says, *"Therefore, remember how you have heard and received . . . keep it and repent."*

The word "remember" means "to constantly call to mind." The church at Sardis is to constantly be thinking about how they responded to the good news of Jesus Christ when they first heard.

The cure for this nearly dead church was to keep in mind the way or how they had first responded to the truth of God. Jesus says "hold on to it firmly . . . to keep it."

That goes for those of us who are followers of Jesus today. My own decision to follow Jesus was one of those dramatic spiritual battles where the heavens opened up and I could hear the angels rejoicing...

Well, maybe not quite that dramatic. But I can still clearly remember the intense spiritual struggle that went on before I made the decision to follow Christ. When I finally submitted my life to Christ, I instantly knew that my life was changed. We are to remember how we first responded to Christ. Here are a couple of verses that will explain what I am talking about.

Colossians 2:6: *"And now, just as you accepted Christ Jesus as your Lord, you must continue to follow him."*

1 Thessalonians 2:13: *"Therefore, we never stop thanking God that when you received his message from us, you didn't think of our words as mere human ideas. You accepted what we said as the very word of God—which, of course, it is. And this word continues to work in you who believe."*

We are to remember our calling and continue to follow Jesus. How? Through daily repentance. There is that "R" word again. I wonder if this word repentance is kind of a bygone practice in Christianity today. We feel that as Christians today we can either take it or leave it. Instead of truly repenting we think the meaning of repentance is just saying we're sorry and then move on.

Some people today believe that all they have to do to get into heaven is to simply pray a prayer and ask Jesus into their lives. You don't have to make any life change because Jesus "paid it all." Well, Jesus did pay it all, but there is more to becoming a Christian than just praying a prayer. It requires real life change. In his book *I Call It Heresy*, R.A. Tozer expressed his feelings about this heresy that has crept into evangelical circles.

Tozer writes, " . . . *feeling that a notable heresy has come into being throughout evangelical Christian circles— the widely-accepted concept that we humans can choose to accept Christ only because we need him as Savior and that we have the right to postpone our obedience to him as Lord as long as we want to!*" Tozer goes on to state, "*that salvation apart from obedience is unknown in the sacred scriptures.*" [57]

Christians today are basically telling Jesus, "*I am really thankful for you dying for me, but if you could excuse me, I would like to get on with my life and I will see you in heaven.*" Do you think Jesus finds this acceptable? This is not the repentance that Jesus is talking about here in Revelation.

Repentance in this verse is the Greek word "meta-noēson," which is an essential element of true conversion and is not optional. A great definition of repentance would be: "a godly sorrow for one's sin along with a resolution to turn from it." Jesus proclaimed: "*Repent and believe in the Gospel*" Mark 1:15.

That is the message to the believers in Sardis and it is still his message for us today. And then he warns, "*If you don't wake up, I will come to you suddenly, as unexpected as a thief.*"

Remember earlier in this chapter I mentioned that Sardis fell because the enemy scaled an "impenetrable" cliff and captured the city? The enemy snuck into the city like a thief. It was totally unexpected.

Jesus is warning them in terms of something they were familiar with. Twice in the history of Sardis the enemy came like a thief in the night. Jesus lifted this right out of history and said, "if you don't get your act together, I'm going to come into your life like a thief in a night. He talks about His coming suddenly when no one expects in His

Olivet Discourse in Matthew 24:42-44. 42"*Therefore be on the alert, for you do not know which day your Lord is coming. 43 But be sure of this, that if the head of the house had known at what time of the night the thief was coming, he would have been on the alert and would not have allowed his house to be broken into.* [44] *For this reason you also must be ready; for the Son of Man is coming at an hour when you do not think He will."*

There is no warning with the Lord.

When we were kids, my younger brother and I slept in the same room. My parents would tuck us in and sing to us before the lights went out. Did we take that as a signal to rollover and go to sleep? Of course not. We would continue to horse-around, laughing and giggling. This would go on until my dad would yell down the hall telling us to go to sleep. This scenario would go on for about a half hour. Suddenly the bedroom door would burst open... judgment! My dad never came down the hall going, "I am coming down the hall now to spank your little bottoms with the wooden spoon! I am just outside your door!" No, there was no warning, no sound. Out of nowhere he would strike. The same is going to happen to the church in Sardis. The warning has already been given and God is about to burst through their door...judgment.

But now a promise is given to the individuals who are faithful to the Lord: Look at verses 4-5: 4 *"Yet there are some in the church in Sardis who have not soiled their clothes with evil. They will walk with me in white, for they are worthy. 5 All who are victorious will be clothed in white. I will never erase their names from the Book of Life, but I*

183

will announce before my Father and his angels that they are mine."

What we have in Sardis is a church full of unspiritual, dead people. The Greek word for some is the word *"oligas,"* which means slight, or small. God always has a few. Not everybody bows the knee to Baal, right? Romans 11:1-5 reminds us of that.

Take a look at these two verses and see the three promises for those who are victorious in their walk with Christ. First, they will "walk in white" meaning they will be clothed in white.

"Soiled garments" possibly speaks of the contamination by living life to the standards of the world, prevalent in any society. More precisely, it refers to the unrighteousness of men in immorality, apostasy, idolatry, or of their own religious works of righteousness.

But Jesus says some of you who do not soil their garments will walk alongside me in white. You are worthy to walk with me. What great words to hear from the Lord Jesus Christ.

Garments in scripture have reference to character. Historians tell us that it was not uncommon for people to put on clean clothes when they went to worship their pagan deities. That practice still goes on today in churches all across America. When I was a kid people would put on their "Sunday best" before attending church. Even though it has gotten a lot more casual today, a majority of people still put on clean clothes when they attend a church service. At least you would hope they would.

White garments in scripture are usually a symbol of redemption and purity.

During the transfiguration, Jesus is described as wearing such garments: 2 *"As the men watched, Jesus' appearance was transformed so that his face shone like the sun, and his clothes became as white as light."* Matthew 17:2

" *. . . and his clothes became dazzling white, far whiter than any earthly bleach could ever make them.* " Mark 9:3

Even un-fallen angels are seen in scripture as wearing white (Matthew 28, Mark 16).

The 24 elders seated around the throne of God were clothed in white garments (Revelation 4:4). In the seventh chapter of this book we read of a great multitude of people who come out of the Great Tribulation and who have *"washed their robes and made them white in the blood of the Lamb"* (Revelation 7:14).

So clearly, white garments are a sign of being redeemed, being saved by the grace of God. These people were "worthy," not because they have lived good moral lives but because they had washed away their sins in the blood of the Lamb. They were worthy because God had imparted to them the righteousness of Christ.

Secondly, their names will not be removed from the Book of Life. The million-dollar question is *your name in the Book of Life?*

I am going to spend some time on this. It is vital to your eternal destination that you do not miss this point.

The current polls from ABC News tell us that about 83 percent of Americans consider themselves to be Christian. [58] (Yes, depending on the source you read this number will vary) The question is are all of these "Christians" going to go to heaven? I would guess not. I could safely venture to say that a large percentage of them will not see the gates of heaven. The reason being, not all of those 83 percent are really Christian. Many Americans who believe they are Christians will be surprised to find out—sadly when it is too late—that their names are not written in the Book of Life. Those are not my words, but the words of our Lord Jesus Christ.

Let's take a look at Matthew 7: 21-23. 21 *"Not everyone who calls out to me, 'Lord! Lord!' will enter the Kingdom of Heaven. Only those who actually do the will of my Father in heaven will enter. 22 On judgment day many will say to me, 'Lord! Lord! We prophesied in your name and cast out demons in your name and performed many miracles in* your name.' 23 *But I will reply, 'I never knew you. Get away from me, you who break God's laws.'"*

How about Luke 13:22-24? 22 *Jesus went through the towns and villages, teaching as he went, always pressing on toward Jerusalem. 23 Someone asked him, "Lord, will only a few be saved?" He replied, 24 "Work hard to enter the narrow door to God's Kingdom, for many will try to enter but will fail."*

According to this next verse in Matthew 7:13-14, it sounds like only a few will be saved. 13 *"You can enter God's Kingdom only through the narrow gate. The highway to hell is broad and its gate is wide for the many who choose that way. 14 But the gateway to life is very narrow and the road is difficult, and only a few ever find it."*

I'll admit that these are some pretty tough verses. Why? Because we have simply sold people a false Gospel, i.e. "pray this prayer...accept Jesus into your heart...invite Christ into your life." It's basically modern evangelism built on sinking sand and it runs the risk of disillusioning millions of souls. I am amazed how many people believe they are Christian just because they were born in the United States or born Baptist.

The question I want to ask you is this: Are you truly a follower of Jesus Christ? If you were to die today, do you have the assurance that you will spend eternity in

His presence? Was there a point in your life where you recognized that you were a sinner and in need of Jesus' redemptive grace? Has the Spirit of God come into your life and changed you? Has there been continual spiritual change in your life? Is there evidence of the fruit of the Spirit in your life? When you sin are you sorry about your sin? Are you repentant, meaning are you trying to change your unwanted behavior? Do you spend time alone with God reading His Word? Do you spend time in prayer? Are you concerned about the spiritual and physical well being of others? Are you actively involved with other believers on a weekly basis? Have you ever shared your love for God with others? The problem is that many people have prayed the prayer somewhere in their past. They may have grown up in the church and may even show some semblance of morality. (I know a lot of non-Christians who live very moral lives) They are living for themselves and are more concerned about things of this world. Paul tells us in 2 Timothy 3:5 that these people:

" ... *will act religious, but they will reject the power that could make them godly.*"

John 2:23-24 states: "*Many trusted in his name, Jesus, however, would not entrust himself to them.*"

Is it possible for people to say they believe in Jesus, to say they have accepted Jesus, but they are not saved and will not enter the kingdom of heaven? Is that possible? Absolutely, it's possible. It's not just possible; it is probable.

We live in a day of "rampant easy-believism" that creates cultural Christians who do not truly know the risen Christ. They have never considered the cost of following Jesus. If they have, they chose the easy road. We must be biblically clear about saving faith, lest any of us lead people down a very dangerous and potentially damning road of spiritual deception.

From the previous verses it sounds like it can be difficult to enter heaven. It isn't about just praying a prayer and then doing what you want. It involves bending your knee and your will to Jesus Christ. It involves living a life of repentance. When a person decides to follow Christ, there is a universal forgiveness of sin. Our sins are forgiven past, present and future. But there is also a personal daily asking for forgiveness from our hourly and daily sins (1 John 1:9). We have to live in obedience to his Word.

5 *"But those who obey God's word truly show how completely they love him. That is how we know we are living in him. 6 Those who say they live in God should live their lives as Jesus did."* 1 John 2:5-6

I want you to be completely sure that when the day comes for you to go into eternity, that your name will be in the Book of Life.

I have had several of my atheist friends ask me, "*How can you be so sure about eternity*? Doesn't God back in Exodus 32:33 say to Moses, . . . *I will erase the name of everyone who has sinned against me*." Isn't that a contradiction? Then in Revelation Jesus says He is not going to erase our names from the book. It's a good question. And, honestly, it is not a contradiction.

In the Exodus passage God does not say specifically the "Book of Life." He is referring to these peoples' death—in my vernacular—they will become extinct. He is going to remove them from this earth. God is not talking about the book of the redeemed. Your salvation was sealed before the world began. God may take your life because of sin, but He will never take your salvation if you are a believer.

In the days of the New Testament, those in charge of the city would keep a register of those who lived within. If you died or committed a serious crime and were banished, your name was erased from the book or register.

Later during the Reformation and the various "inquisitions" by the Catholic Church those found guilty were not only excommunicated from the faith, but they were tortured, executed and then sentenced to an eternity in

Hell (Not sure how they could really do that...sentence people to Hell).

If you are a follower of Jesus, He says He will never erase your name from the Book of Life. That word *never*, is the strongest negative in the Greek language. It should be translated, "I will never, ever, under any circumstances, blot out your name from the book of life." What wonderful reassurance!

And finally . . . "*I will announce before my Father and his angels that they are mine.*"

This verse reminds me of Jesus' words back in Mathew 10:32:

"*Everyone who acknowledges me publicly here on earth, I will also acknowledge before my Father in heaven.*"

Jesus is saying that He will announce or literally confess the "overcomers" name before the Father and the angels. This is reward language.

The word "confess" is the Greek word "homologēsō" which means, "to acknowledge, claim, profess." Jesus will acknowledge faithful believers before the Father and before His angels.

Then Jesus closes this letter with the familiar words, "*Anyone with ears to hear must listen to the Spirit and understand what he is saying to the churches.*"

A brilliant young pianist was giving his very first concert. As the final chord of his flawless performance reverberated in the hall, the audience rose to its feet and broke out in thunderous applause. Only one member of the audience remained seated, clapping politely, but without particular enthusiasm. Tears welled up in the young pianist's eyes. His head dropped slightly as he left the stage in utter defeat. The stage manager in the great hall was a sensitive and observant man who had noticed the lone gentleman and saw how this cool response affected the star performer. "Son," he said, "you're a hit! Everyone was overwhelmed. The critic from the Times was in tears. By morning you'll be famous. Don't let one guy get you down."

"You don't understand," the dejected young man replied. "That man was my piano teacher. It only matters what he thinks." [59]

I have done a lot of things in my life that others would consider great. I have been applauded and rewarded for my efforts. Honestly, the only thing that really matters in this life is what I have done for Jesus Christ. Someday we will all stand before the Savior and we will be judged for what we have done for Him. The world can applaud my life, but it only matters to me what my Savior has to say about my life. I don't want to disappoint Him.

His message to the believer's in Sardis—I know you are dead. You *may* look alive; you may be doing great ministry, but in all honesty, you are dead. You're going to be judged; you can't hide in the church. The Lord knows you, He sees you, He knows your condition, He knows that you're dead, and He's coming in judgment. Wake up! Repent from your sins and start obeying my Word and follow me.

That is God's message to the believer's in Sardis.

Questions for Thoughtful Discussion

1. Does it ever bother you that Jesus knows everything you will think, say or do? Does knowing that affect the way you live?

2. How can a church be dead? Do you attend a "dead church?" How would you know if your church was dead? What do you think Jesus is looking for in His church?

3. What makes a person dead spiritually?

4. What do you think about my friend's statement that you can run a successful church ministry without God? How about the Christian life? Can you live it without the power of the Holy Spirit?

   Let's pretend that the Holy Spirit left you one day (just pretend, OK?) Would you even notice that He was gone? Would you even miss Him?

5. What does it mean to follow Jesus?

6. Do you know for certain that if you were to die today that you would spend eternity in heaven? Are you sure? What are your thoughts on those tough statement by Jesus? Matthew 7:14-14; 21:33; Luke 13:22-24

7. How would you explain to someone what it means to live and walk by the Spirit of God?

8. Are you living a life of repentance and obedience? Is the fruit of the Spirit evident in your life? Are you concerned for the poor, the hungry and those who don't know Jesus?

Chapter 7

THE CHURCH AT PHILADELPHIA —
Don't Give Up

A young teenage son complained to his father about how hard life was. "Life seems to be just one problem after another," he said, "sometimes I'm so tired of the struggle."

His father took him into the kitchen where he filled three pots with water and then placed each on a high fire. Soon the pots came to a boil. In one of the pots he placed carrots, in the second, eggs, and in the last, ground coffee beans. He let them sit and boil without saying a word. The son impatiently waited, wondering what he was doing. After awhile the father went over and turned off the burners. He fished out the carrots and eggs and placed them into separate bowls. He then poured the coffee into a third bowl.

Turning to his son he asked, "OK, what do you see?"

"Carrots, eggs, and coffee," the son replied.

He told his son to get closer and to feel the carrots. The son did and noted that they were soft. He then asked him to take an egg and break it. After pulling off the shell the son observed the egg was hard-boiled. Finally, he asked the son to sip the coffee. He smiled, as he tasted its rich flavor. Afterwards the son asked, "OK . . . so what does all this mean?"

The dad explained that each of them had faced the same adversity—boiling water—but each reacted differently. The carrot went in strong, hard, and unrelenting, but after being subjected to the boiling water, it softened and became weak and mushy. The egg was fragile. Its thin outer shell had protected its liquid interior, but after sitting through the boiling water, its inside hardened. The ground coffee beans were unique, however. By being in the boiling water they changed the water.

The father then asked his son, "When hard times and adversity strikes, which of these three items identifies you?"

How are you going to react to the hard times? That's is a question that each of us has to figure out at some point in our lives. How are we going to react when adversity and hard times hit us? We are going to take a look at a church that went through some tough times.

Most everyone knows that our historic American city of Philadelphia, Pennsylvania has the same name as the church to which we come to in this chapter. Philadelphia of course means "City of Brotherly Love."

This biblical city was located about 28 miles southeast of the city of Sardis. It was the youngest of the seven cities whose churches are addressed in these letters.

King Attallus of Pergamum, whose nickname was Philadelphus, which means "lover of a brother," founded Philadelphia about 150 BC King Attallus was known for the admiration and love he had for his brother, Eumenes, and he named this city in honor of him. The city actually stood on a hill, looking over a long valley. Volcanic cliffs encircled this valley and the land was rich and fertile from the volcanic residue. The downside of living in an area with so many volcanoes was of course earthquakes. Because of its location, the city was in constant danger of earthquakes and experienced aftershocks as an everyday occurrence. An earthquake in 17 AD along with Sardis and other cities in that locality eventually destroyed the city. This earthquake was recorded by the Roman historians Tacitus and Pliny the Elder. Pliny called it "the greatest earthquake in human memory"[60]

Most of the other cities recovered rather quickly from the disaster, but the after-shocks continued in

Philadelphia for quite a number of years. As a result, many of its inhabitants chose to live in huts outside the city in the open surrounding countryside. Tiberius Caesar helped Philadelphia to recover from the earthquake, and out of gratitude the city changed its name to Neocaesarea (New Caesar), and for a while it bore that name. So the city would have to been rebuilt by the time John was writing in about 95-96 AD

William Barclay points out that this city had a special "mission." Philadelphia could be called a "missionary city." Philadelphia was situated near the borders of Mysia, Lydia and Phrygia. It was a border town Like Nogales in Arizona or Tijuana south of San Diego. It was founded with the deliberate intention that it could bring the Greek culture and the Greek language to Lydia and Phrygia. It worked so well by AD 19, the Lydian's had forgotten their own Lydian language and considered themselves Greeks. [61]

The city was located on a major trade route. At one time during the Byzantine era historians tell us it was the single greatest trade route in Asia Minor. There is not a lot of information on this city. So what about the church in Philadelphia?

Again, there's not a whole lot of information except what we read in this letter. There's no mention of it anywhere in Scripture other than here in Revelation. There was no condemnation from Jesus to this church.

Let's get into our text for this chapter: "*And to the angel of the church in Philadelphia write*: '*The words of the holy one, the true one, who has the key of David, who opens and no one will shut, who shuts and no one opens . . .*'"

Notice the difference in this opening? In all the other letters, our Lord uses symbols to describe himself that come from the vision John had of him, recorded in Chapter 1. In this letter, however, Jesus makes no reference to that vision. He uses other titles to describe himself. He tells the readers in this letter "who" He is and "what" He does.

Jesus is holy and true. He is without flaw or blemish because He is God incarnate. In the Greek, Jesus is literally "set apart and genuine." What Jesus does is hold the key of David. So, what is the key of David? To discover the answer to this question you will have to go back to Isaiah chapter 22. Jesus is referring to an incident from way, way back.

In the days of King Hezekiah there was a treasurer over the house of David (what we would call today a comptroller or chief-of-staff). His name was Shebna. He was a very prideful man and he seems to have been in favor of an alliance with Egypt and Syria. Because of that, he fell into disfavor with God. Listen to what God says he is going to do with him.

"...*The Lord is about to hurl you away, mighty man. He is going to grab you, crumple you into a ball, and toss you away into a distant, barren land. There you will die, and your glorious chariots will be broken and useless. You are a disgrace to your master!*" Isaiah 22:17-18

This probably seemed ridiculous to Shebna at the time because he believed himself to be safe and secure in his position. Like most American politicians, he thought he had job security. He even had a sepulcher hewn out for himself as a monument to his greatness.

Some Jewish historians believe Shebna contracted leprosy and was forced from the court and eventually the nation because the disease was seen as a direct judgment of God (There is some evidence to indicate he was taken away to Babylon). If this is what happened, then God's judgment was complete. A godly man named Eliakim would replace him. This gave Eliakim access to all of David's riches.

Isaiah 22:22 goes on to say, "*I will give him the key to the house of David—the highest position in the royal court. When he opens doors, no one will be able to close them; when he closes doors, no one will be able to open them.*"

So the key indicates control or authority; therefore, having the Key of David would give one control of David's domain, i.e., Jerusalem, the City of David, and the kingdom of Israel.

Jesus is referring back to the passage in Isaiah and applies it to himself. Notice that Jesus didn't say "a" key but "*the*" key. Jesus holds the master key. Now he tells the church, beginning in verse 8, how he will use this power to open and shut. "'*I know your works. Behold, I have set before you an open door, which no one is able to shut. I know that you have but little power, and yet you have kept my word and have not denied my name.*'"

The holy and true Lord Jesus Christ knows everything there is to know. He is saying to the church in Philadelphia that He knows what they are really like. And yet, because He knows everything, He commends them. Jesus says that He has opened a door, which no one can shut. I truly believe the Lord can open the doors of ministry and service of the local church as He wishes. This reminds me of the apostle Paul's second journey. From Pisidian Antioch in the region of Phrygia and Galatia, Paul intends to make his way straight west into the Roman province of Asia, about 150 miles to Colosse and then 100 or so to Ephesus. The Holy Spirit shut the door.

We are not told how, but the Holy Spirit clearly prevents them from taking that route. This occurs probably before they set off or early in their passage, for they evidently turn northward almost immediately.

Then Paul tried to go into Bithynia, on the southern shore of the Black Sea, but was again, shut out. Again there is no indication of the means that the Holy Spirit uses. Paul evidently takes this negative guidance to mean that he must push the mission farther west, across the Aegean to Greece. But when he came to Troas, more properly Alexandria Troas, he had a vision of a man from Macedonia, and he learned that the Lord had opened a door for him into Europe.

In First Corinthians 16:9, Paul says of Ephesus, the capital of Asia, "*There is a wide-open door for a great work here, although many oppose me.*" So the door that had been closed to him once was now opened to him by the Lord.

Doors are opening in countries that we would have never expected. Doors have opened to the Gospel in countries like Russia, Romania, Poland and the former East Germany. There are even predictions that within the next 15 years, China will be open to the Gospel. As a matter of fact, there are predictions that within 15 years China could become the most Christian nation. [62] These are doors, which had been closed for decades. Even in the most communist and anti-Christian country of Albania, the church is growing. Of course the doors are closing also in many Islamic countries like Iran, Afghanistan and Egypt to just name a few. (Just a side note: Despite the Iranian government's ongoing crackdown of Christians living in the primarily Islamic country, the number of Muslims converting to Christianity is growing at an explosive rate. The house church movement within Iran is part of that revival and has triggered "many secret meetings." The growth in the number of Christians is happening in all regions, but mostly in larger cities).[63] The important point is this: God still sits on the throne and allows doors to open and doors to close as he wishes.

Not only is this true in countries being opened to the Gospel, but is can also be true in each of our lives. God opens doors and He closes doors. Maybe some of you have had this experience in your life.

Jesus is literally saying to them . . . *"I have set before you an open door, which no one is able to shut. I know that you have but little power, and yet you have kept my word and have not denied my name."*

I think this teaches us something very important. The church in Philadelphia met certain conditions and the

Lord opened the door for them to minister. What conditions did they meet? He says they had a little power.

The Greek word for power is *dunamin*. We get our word for dynamite from it. I believe the Lord is talking here about spiritual power and not strength. It is a power that is obtained only by faith. What do I mean by that? Let me give you a quick example.

A few years back I was coaching pole vault at Hillsboro High School in Hillsboro, Oregon. One day near the end of track season, I was approached by a parent of one of the kids. He knew that I had a background in Young Life and asked if I would to help start a club in Hillsboro. There was just a slight problem; there was no money, no committee, no staff and no kids. We were off to a great start. There were just two people who had been praying for over eight years for God to start a Young Life Club in the local school in Hillsboro. To make a long story short, in fewer than four months (mid-September) we had a club running with over a hundred kids in attendance. I had more staff and volunteers than I could handle. We had a committee and had started raising funds and eventually hired a full time leader. People often ask me how I was able to pull all that off in just four short months? To be totally honest, I have no clue; it just happened and it was all God. I just took a step of faith and God did the rest. God has done that several times in my life. It just takes a little faith—and a little dynamite—to do great things for God.

Remember God promised that His Spirit would come and reside within us (1 Corinthians 3:16). Because we have the Spirit, we have His power. Because we have His power, we are able to obey His Word. And because we are obedient to His Word, we will not deny the character of Christ in our lives. That is why He was commending the church in Philadelphia.

Let me say something before we move on. This may be one of the most important things I say in this whole book. You need to understand that the "Spiritual Life" is not equivalent to the "Christian life." You need to fully understand this. The Christian life is being rightly related to the Son of God, and the spiritual life is being rightly related to the Spirit of God. Thus our problem! There are many Christians and church leaders who are not "spiritual."

Let me ask you a question. What did the Holy Spirit do for you today? Okay, you were really busy today so how about yesterday? Last week? What difference would it make if God removed the Holy Spirit from of your life today? Would He be missed? How long would it take you to miss Him? Would you even notice? When was the last time the concept of the Holy Spirit even crossed your mind?

If you have trouble answering these questions or if it has been awhile since you even thought about the Holy Spirit, you need to put this book down and repent of your sin. How can you even function as a Christian without the power of the Holy Spirit in your life? You can't; it is impossible.

Let me ask you another question. Is the Spirit of God at work in your life? Does your life daily exhibit the fruit of the Spirit? Are you obedient to His Word? John, in chapter 14 of his Gospel, writes this:

"If anyone loves Me, he will keep My word; and My Father will love him, and We will come to him and make Our abode with him. He who does not love Me does not keep My words . . . " John 14:23, 24

That's the characteristic of a believer. The reason the "church" in the US is in such moral decline today is many Christians have truly forgotten what it means to be empowered by the Spirit of God. The church in Philadelphia was spot on! They had just a little faith, and they kept His Word and refused to deny him. Please don't miss what I am saying here.

Look at verse 9:*"Look, I will force those who belong to Satan's synagogue—those liars who say they are Jews but are not—to come and bow down at your feet. They will acknowledge that you are the ones I love."*

Here we see the reference again to the "synagogue of Satan. " Jesus mentions them back in Revelation 2:9 in His letter to the church of Smyrna. It refers to certain Jews who claimed to be spiritual descendants of Abraham but, in actuality, were only his physical descendants; their attitude towards the truth of God was far removed from Abraham's faith. Remember back in John 8:44 where Jesus tells the Pharisees (the Jewish religious leaders) that their father was the devil? So here in the city of Philadelphia, as in the city of Smyrna, Jesus refers to this Jewish opposition as "the synagogue of Satan." For a little more enlightenment on this subject, you could read Romans 9:6-8.

They were not children of God regardless of their claims and religiosity. Jesus says that He will make these Jews *"come and bow down at your feet."* Bowing down at someone's feet was the ancient posture of a humbled, defeated enemy. I'm going to bring these enemies in and they're going to bow down at your feet. So what does this mean?

My theory is simply this: Jesus is saying that some of these Jews will come to a saving faith through these believers in Philadelphia.

Let's move on. Verse 10: *"Because you have kept my word about patient endurance, I will keep you from the hour of trial that is coming on the whole world, to try those who dwell on the earth."*

This is kind of a wacky translation. What this literally says is, *"Because you have kept the word of my patient endurance."* What does that mean? I like how the NIV translates this verse, *"You have kept my command to endure patiently."* Just as Christ endured patiently during his ministry on earth, He is asking the believer's in Philadelphia to do the same. I think this was what Paul was intending in his prayer for the believers in Thessalonica: *"May the Lord lead your hearts into a full understanding and expression of the love of God and the patient endurance that comes from Christ."* 2 Thessalonians 3:5

I believe that Jesus is telling the believers in Philadelphia, "Since you have been obedient, since you have been patient and have endured, I will also keep you from the hour of trial that is going to come upon the whole world to test those who live on the earth." Basically you have passed the tests set before you; I will keep you from the future test that will come.

The next question is what "trial or testing" is He promising to keep them from? It could have been some simple, historical reference to literally sparing the church in Philadelphia from some kind of local trouble or persecution. It could have even pertained to all the times the nearby volcanoes erupted and the earthquake destroyed their city. But whatever it was, Jesus promised to keep them from it. But I believe there is more to it than just a literal, historical sense. I believe Jesus was talking about events that would happen in the future.

Let's look at this verse again. "*I will keep you out of the hour of trial that is coming on the whole world, to try those who dwell on the earth.*"

I believe this passage is talking to the *ekklesia*, the church. In these two chapters in Revelation, Jesus is talking to the church as a whole. This trial that is coming is not just going to affect just the local church but the whole world.

This coming event is sometime in the future, and will be limited in its time, and it will be worldwide. Let me see if I can explain it without losing you. I need to get into a little Greek here to explain. The Greek word for trial or testing is the Greek word *peirasmou*. It can be defined as simply a trial or testing. To understand the exact meaning of the word we have to understand the context. Here the context shows us the reference is to a very specific world-wide testing or tribulation. Because it is *the* hour of testing, it shows a very specific time of testing. This testing will be for the whole world to experience. This test or trial is for a certain category of people defined as "those who dwell upon the earth." As used in Revelation, "those who dwell upon the earth" can be used basically as a technical term for unbelievers. "This hour of trial," is sometimes referred to as "the Tribulation," which refers to the time of wrath and judgment described in chapters 6-19 of Revelation. This is the same as Daniel's Seventieth Week (Dan. 9:27) and the time of "Jacob's trouble" described by Jeremiah as being unprecedented in its judgment (Jer. 30:7).

This is a clear reference to what our Lord himself calls in Matthew 24 "the Great Tribulation" -- a time of distress that will come upon the whole world, the likes of which has never been known before in human history. Whether you are a dispensationalist, post-trib, mid-trib or pre-trib, Republican or Democrat, this statement of Jesus is quite clear. There is coming a time in the near future when all hell will break loose. We may think things are bad now, but it is nothing compared to what is to come. But now my "pre-trib" dispensational leanings are going to be revealed. I truly believe that the promise to the church is specifically that it is to be delivered from this hour of the tribulation.

Actually the word is not "from," but "out of" the very time of the trial! This is one of the clearest promises in the Bible of the "catching away" of the church before the great tribulation begins. It is a promise of the departure of the church, which Paul describes so vividly in First Thessalonians 4. "16 *For the Lord himself will descend from heaven with a cry of command, with the voice of an archangel, and with the sound of the trumpet of God. And the dead in Christ will rise first. 17 Then we who are alive, who are left, will be caught up together with them in the clouds to meet the Lord in the air, and so we will always be with the Lord. 18 Therefore encourage one another with these words.*" 1 Thessalonians 4:16-17

That is a very wonderful promise, and many signs indicate that the world may be moving that direction. Jesus has just been describing a time when the greatest trial that the earth will ever experience will be the terrible great tribulation. As I mentioned earlier, Jesus has described this period of time very clearly in his Olivet Discourse, in Matthew 24. In this passage we have a terrible picture of the sun being darkened, the moon not giving its light, stars falling from heaven and men's hearts failing as they look in fear on the things coming to pass upon the earth. It is in relationship to that event that Jesus says He is coming soon. As the world nears that final, climactic upheaval we should hear again His promise that He is coming soon. He himself said, "*Now when these things begin to take place, straighten up and raise your heads, because your redemption is drawing near.*" Luke 21:28. It is in that connection that He utters this promise to come soon. More on this in a moment.

I will say this, we Christians are to be looking forward to His return (Luke 12:35-50; Mark 13:33-37; Matthew 24:42-44; 2 Peter 3:10-12). I think the Church has pretty much forgotten this aspect of our faith. We are so busy worrying about the here and now, building up our little kingdoms, that we have forgotten He is returning. Are you looking forward to his return? Are you ready?

Then the Lord adds this in verse 11, "*I am coming soon. Hold fast what you have, so that no one may seize your crown.*"

His coming is promised to be "soon" but that is not exactly the best translation from the Greek to English. The best definition would be the word "quickly." This means "suddenly, unexpectedly, without announcement" and not necessarily soon. It implies immanency. So what does Jesus mean by "hold fast?" Back in chapter 2 verse 25 Jesus told the church in Thyatira to "hold fast until I come." Hold fast means being faithful, persevering and enduring. When Jesus returns we will be examined and rewarded for what we have done in his name. If we fail in our service to the Lord we can lose our crown. What does John mean by saying, "hold fast what you have, so that no one will take your crown?"

I see two possibilities.

One, it could refer to rewards, which are lost and given to others because we failed to hold fast. Remember Paul's words to the Corinthians: "*Do you not know that those who run in a race all run, but only one receives the prize? Run in such a way that you may win.*" 1 Corinthians 9:24

Two, it could refer to rewards lost because of the evil influences we might allow to hinder us in the race of life. Romans 8:5-9 tells us that in order to do this we need to walk according to the Spirit and not the flesh.

5 "*For those who are according to the flesh set their minds on the things of the flesh, but those who are according to the Spirit, the things of the Spirit. 6 For the mind set on the flesh is death, but the mind set on the Spirit is life and peace, 7 because the mind set on the flesh is hostile toward God; for it does not subject itself to the law of God, for it is not even able to do so, 8 and those who are in the flesh cannot please God. 9 However, you are not in the flesh but in the Spirit, if indeed the Spirit of God dwells in you. But if anyone does not have the Spirit of Christ, he does not belong to Him.*"

I personally believe that both concepts are true. We need to make sure we do not lose the crowns that are given to us. Remember that we do not earn these crowns. We need to remain faithful and persevere. And if we do

Jesus makes this promise in verse 12. "*The one who con-quers, I will make him a pillar in the temple of my God. Never shall he go out of it, and I will write on him the name of my God, and the name of the city of my God, the new Jerusalem, which comes down from my God out of heaven, and my own new name.*"

Again the person who overcomes or who conquers will be blessed. The first promise is they will be made a pillar in the temple of God. "*I will make him a pillar in the temple of my God.*" When you visit or see pictures of ancient ruins you will notice that often all that is left standing are the pillars. A pillar is a symbol of strength and permanence. In Galatians, the Apostle Paul refers to Peter, James and John as "pillars" of the church; the church rested upon them in some sense as they were imparting guidance and knowledge to fellow believers. Those who have overcome will have as a reward a special ministry as a permanent and prominent fixture in the temple of God (Ephesians 2:20-22). In the Jerusalem temple, which was destroyed in 70 A. D., there were two great pillars in front of the building, one called Jachin (which means "established, permanent"), and the other Boaz ("strength"). Pillars are thus symbols of strength and permanence. "Never again will he leave it," Jesus says.

Once a builder puts a pillar in place, it does not move from that building. Jesus assures these believers that they will never be removed from their place of preeminence in the eternal temple.

Finally, Jesus promises those who overcome that they will have three special names. Jesus says he will write upon the overcomer three names.

The first is the name of my God (signifying His ownership). I love that thought. God loves me and wants to write his name on me.

We do that today; we write our names on things that we own to show possession. I belong to God.

The second: the city of God, the New Jerusalem (which signifies citizenship in the heavenly city, (Ps 87:5-6).

Finally, Christ's new name (the full revelation of His character and special intimacy with Christ in His kingdom). For those of us who overcome—the true followers of Jesus Christ—if we hang in there until the end, Jesus promises to make it worth our while. Let me show you what Romans 8:14-17 says: 14 *For all who are led by the Spirit of God are sons of God.* 15 *For you did not receive the spirit of slavery to fall back into fear, but you have received the Spirit of adoption as sons, by whom we cry, "Abba! Father!"* 16 *The Spirit himself bears witness with our spirit that we are children of God,* 17 *and if children, then* heirs—*heirs of God and fellow heirs with Christ, provided we suffer with him in order that we may also be glorified with him."*

And if that is not enough, Paul goes on: 18 *For I consider that the sufferings of this present time are not worth comparing with the glory that is to be revealed to us."*

Did you get all that? What a glorious future awaits the true follower of Jesus Christ. If we can just hang on and endure all this temporary crap the world throws at us, our eternal reward will be well worth it. Amen?

And to top it all off, Revelation 22:4 tells us that not only will He write His name on us, but we will finally be able to see His face. We will be able to look into the actual face of God. What a great future awaits those who stay true to God.

Finally in verse 13: *"He who has an ear, let him hear what the Spirit says to the churches."*

Stop! Listen up! Listen to the Spirit of God! Read and think carefully through these letters! Pay very careful attention to them, because they are spelling out your future destiny.

Questions for Thoughtful Discussion

1. How do you react to difficulties in your life?

2. I am going to ask you those questions again on allowing the Spirit of God to control your life. What did the Holy Spirit do for you today? How about last week? (I know this is unscriptural but) What difference would it make if God removed the Holy Spirit from of your life today? Would He be missed? How long would it take you to miss Him? Would you even notice if the Spirit of God left you? When was the last time the concept of the Holy Spirit even crossed your mind? These are questions that cannot be ignored or taken lightly.

3. As a follower of Jesus Christ, we will experience some amazing things in our future with Christ. Just check out the promises at the end of each chapter. Take some time to investigate the future promises that will belong to the believer. It will amaze you when you find out what the true believer will experience in the future Kingdom as well as in the New Heaven and New Earth.

Chapter 8

THE CHURCH AT LAODICEA —
"You Make Me Sick"

For years I used to drive around town with a Big Gulp[64] in the cup holder between the seats of my Chevy pickup truck. It was second nature for me while driving to just reach down, take a drink of my soda and then replace it without missing a beat. One day my wife Wendy and I must have taken the truck together somewhere since she left her grande hazelnut latte in my truck. No big deal. Normally we drove Wendy's car since it was cheaper and more convenient to drive. A few days later I got back into my truck to go to work. As was my habit, I reached down between the seats, grabbed my cup and took a big swallow only to immediately spew the contents in my mouth all over the dashboard and myself. What had I just spit out?

A two-day-old hazelnut vanilla latte that my wife had left in the cup holder between the seats.

Let me add it had been sitting in the hot Arizona sun.

Talk about disgusting. On top of it all I hate coffee. It took days before I could get the taste of that curdled concoction out of my mouth.

The reason I bring this up is the idea of spitting something unpleasant from your mouth will be one of the topics in this passage from Revelation. Let's look at this last church—the church of Laodicea.

Laodicea was the chief city of this entire region. The city was originally known as Diospolis ("the City of Zeus").

Antiochus II Theos founded the city between 261 and 253 BC, and he named it in honor of his wife, Laodice. The early population of the city probably consisted of natives of the area, Hellenized Greeks and veteran soldiers in the army of Antiochus II. The city became part of the kingdom of Pergamon and later passed into Roman hands in 133 BC.

Cicero, the famous Roman orator and statesman, served as governor of the province, residing mostly in Laodicea.

The city of Laodicea was located about 100 miles directly east of Ephesus, the first city to which these seven letters were addressed. It was located in the Lycus River Valley, the southwest area of Phrygia. Originally they had been Phrygian cities, but in the New Testament age they were part of the Roman Province of Asia.

Laodicea was part of a tri-city area, closely associated with the cities of Colossae, which was 10 miles up river on the same side of Laodicea. Hierapolis and Laodicea stood six miles apart on opposite sides of a valley with the Lycus River flowing between them.

With the Lycus Valley being one of the most common routes of travel to the west, people could travel through a valley rather than across mountains. Anytime these cities were on a trade route they became significant.

It was one of the wealthiest cities of the ancient world. As a matter of fact, it was the richest city of the seven churches. Laodicea was a banking center. It was very wealthy apparently because it was on the crossroads of north-south traffic between Sardis and Pergamum and East-West from the Euphrates to Ephesus.

When an earthquake destroyed Laodicea in 60 AD, they refused aid from the Roman Empire and rebuilt the city from their own wealth.

Laodicea was destroyed not once but twice by earth-quakes (17 AD and 60 AD). Both times they rebuilt the city without outside help. Compare that to the destruc-tion caused by hurricane Katrina that devastated New

Orleans and how hard it has been for them to get the city and surrounding area rebuilt.

The remains of the city are basically unexcavated, so most of what we know about the history of the city comes from written sources.

The remains of two theaters, one Greek and one Roman, are on the northeastern slope of the plateau. A large stadium, dedicated by a wealthy citizen to the Roman emperor Vespasian also serves as an amphitheater. It sits on the opposite end of the plateau. This stadium was used for both athletic contests and gladiatorial shows.

The land was fertile in the Lycus River valley and the pastures could hold great flocks of sheep.

The area was a great center for the wool industry and the associated trade of the dyeing of woolen garments. The city was famous especially for the fine black, soft wool of its sheep. In this city they produced what was called the "Laodicean robe." Anybody who was anybody had to have a Laodicean robe.

They raised sheep with both black and white wool. Since the waters around Laodicea were so mineral enriched, they had a bleaching quality about them. So they were able to take the white wool they produced and then they would soak it in the mineral enriched water, it would produce a wool whiter than any other wool produced.

Crucial to any city in the ancient world was its water supply. There were a few local streams in the area but as the population grew, the local streams were inadequate. In fact several of the local streams would completely dry up in the summer. Not only were the local rivers inadequate, but also the water system that the city was using was so mineral enriched that if you drank it, you would get sick.

And so potable water had to be brought in.

Because of the volcanic activity in the area, vents in the earth's surface allowed hot boiling water to reach the surface. Hierapolis, some six miles from Laodicea, was famous for its hot springs. People came from great distances to bathe in those waters, believing they had medicinal powers. The hot spring waters were sent to Laodicea by way of an underground aqueduct. By the time it reached Laodicea, the water was no longer hot; it was lukewarm.

The city of Colossae was some 10 miles away. Colosse was built at the foot of Mt. Cadmus, which towered more than nine thousand feet high. The waters from the snowmelt and fresh springs would bring cold to freezing water to the city of Colosse. So, just as Hierapolis was known for its hot springs, Colosse was known for its cold refreshing waters. Just as people journeyed to Hierapolis to bathe in

223

the hot springs for health purposes, people would travel great distances to vacation in Colosse, where they could invigorate themselves by taking frequent dips into the famous, refreshing, waters of that city. This cold water was also piped into Laodicea by aqueduct; by the time it reached the city, this water was lukewarm as well. This tepid, lukewarm water made getting refreshment in Laodicea difficult. The water piped into Laodicea by aqueduct from the from these two cities was so concentrated with minerals that the Roman engineers designed vents, capped by removable stones, so the aqueduct pipes could periodically be cleared of deposits. [65]

The aqueducts brought the water into the city where it was deposited into a 16-foot collection tower, which then would distribute water throughout the city.

Just a side note about the water system in Laodicea. Any military enemy of Laodicea could sit outside the city, locate the aqueducts and either poison the water, seal it off, then just sit and lay siege to the city until the people ran out of water.

This is probably the reason why Laodicea never became much of a military power. No other city on the Lycus Valley was as dependent on external water supplies as Laodicea.

One great feature about the city was its medical school. Thirteen miles north of the city was a very famous medical school. It was basically established in connection with an ancient temple that was associated with the god identified later by the name of Aesculapius, the god of healing who is still around in old medical literature. You ran into this fellow in the chapter about the city of Pergamum. The medical school had famous teachers, but the thing that was most prominent in the medical school was they developed a certain salve for the eye. And people from all over that part of the world when they had an eye ailment would come to this medical school near Laodicea to get the eye salve that they would then put on their eyes which would bring some measure of comfort and healing.

So as you look at the commercial aspect of Laodicea you see finance, wealth, a city famous for its black and white wool and eye salve. And all three of those industries play a major part in this letter. And actually, so does its water supply.

So what about the church in Laodicea? It was common with many of the Hellenistic cities that there was a prosperous Jewish colony established there well before the Christian era. This was true of Laodicea. There was quite a large population of Jews in Laodicea. Antiochus the Great (not the bad Antiochus IV) favored the Jews. He sent 2000

Jewish families from Babylon and Mesopotamia into the area to settle.[66] Eventually, Jews from Palestine moved into the region for "the wines and baths of Phrygia." It has been estimated that in the year 62 BC, the Jewish population was as high as 50,000. [67] The Christian community in the city seems to have been connected with that of nearby Colossae and Hierapolis. Its congregation was the only one of the seven, with the possible exception of Ephesus, to receive communications both from the apostle Paul and from John of Patmos.

Laodicea is mentioned four times in the New Testament's epistle to the Colossians (Colossians 2:1; 4:13,15,16). Paul in Colossians 2:1 writes: *"For I want you to know how great a struggle I have for you and for those at Laodicea and for all who have not seen me face to face . . . "*

Paul mentions his coworker, Epaphras, who had brought the Christian message to the region (1:7) and was still *"working hard for you and for those at Laodicea and Hierapolis"* (4:13).

He sends greetings *"to the brothers at Laodicea, and to Nympha and the church in her house"* (4:15), requesting that *"after this letter has been read to you, see that it is also read in the church of the Laodiceans and that you in turn read the letter from Laodicea"* (4:16).

If the Colossian epistle is genuinely by Paul, then this would indicate a Christian presence in Laodicea as early as the AD 50's. It would also indicate that Laodicea (like Colossae) was not evangelized by Paul, but possibly by his disciple Epaphras.

It seems that Laodicea was a church with a rich spiritual heritage. So you would think that it would receive great commendation from Jesus. Not so much. What happened? Let's look at this scathing letter to the church in Laodicea.

"And to the angel of the church in Laodicea write: 'The words of the Amen, the faithful and true witness, the beginning of God's creation."

We are all familiar with this word "Amen." We utter it when we close a prayer or when we want to express our agreement with a meaningful statement. For example in some churches, when the pastor says something really profound, you usually hear someone from the back of the congregation shout "Amen." Amen is being said in agreement with a meaningful statement.

But it is also a word that Jesus used frequently. In the more modern versions of the Gospels, he begins many statements with the words, "Truly, truly, I say unto you." The King James Version renders it, "Verily, verily." Actually, in Greek, it is "Amen, Amen." It indicates that Jesus is saying something extremely important. It always marks signifi-cant truth. So when you come to this word in the Gospels, pay careful attention, because Jesus himself is under-scoring that what he is saying is not only true, but also an important truth.

Jesus also calls himself "the faithful and true witness." He has emphasized his truthfulness before in these letters, but here he adds the word "faithful." Jesus not only tells the truth, but he tells all the truth; He is truth. He does not hide anything. He speaks plainly and clearly and reveals the whole truth. He wants this church to understand that.

And then Jesus says He is the origin, the beginning of God's creation. John 1:1-3 tells us: "*In the beginning was the Word, and the Word was with God, and the Word was God. 2 He was in the beginning with God. 3 All things were made through him, and without him was not any thing made that was made.*"

But Jesus made not only the *old* creation, (i.e. the phys-ical universe in which we live, including the great galaxies of space, the planetary system of our sun, and the earth itself) but Jesus will also be the source of the *new* creation. . . us. Paul tells us in Second Corinthians 5:17, " . . . *if anyone is in Christ, he is a new creation. The old has passed away; behold, the new has come.*"

So, as in all the previous letters, our Lord introduces himself in a very significant way. He is the Amen, the faithful and true witness and creator. Not only is He sovereign, but also He is omniscient. He knows their works. He doesn't hold back in telling the believer's in Laodicea how He really feels:

15 *"I know your works: you are neither cold nor hot. Would that you were either cold or hot! 16 So, because you are lukewarm, and neither hot nor cold, I will spit you out of my mouth."*

Jesus is telling the believers in Laodicea that He knows them. He knows their works, their deeds. Just a reminder to us who follow Christ today, our works will always reveal who we truly are. God doesn't miss a thing. Simply put, God knows our works because He knows our hearts. We may be able to fool the people around us, but God is not fooled. He wants the believers in Laodicea to know that.

So what does Jesus mean when he says, *"you are neither cold or hot . . . because you are lukewarm I will spit you out of my mouth."*

I have heard many a message from this passage. I have been studying and teaching the book of Revelation for many years. In my opinion, I believe this is one of the most misunderstood passages in scripture. The only other verse that would beat this passage would be verse 20 in this same chapter.

In order to understand the point or idea of any passage, you have to look at the said passage historically and put it into context. Remember, the book of Revelation is one of the most unique books in all of scripture. It combines the elements of an epistle, prophecy, and apocalyptic literature.

To the church in Laodicea, Jesus gives His infamous "hot," "cold," and "lukewarm" rebuke.

If you read the passage carefully, The rebuke reveals that this particular church had become focused on riches and wealth, as well as pride and spiritual complacency. This is the general context and background of this passage. When you examine the entirety of the preceding verse, Jesus clearly presents what He is specifically speaking of. Jesus says, "I know your works: you are neither cold nor hot."

I think it is very clear that the temperature analogy is directly related to their deeds. Yet, how are we to relate this analogy to "deeds?" The reason I went into such historical background of first century Laodicea is it helps give insight to this issue.

Bear with me for a quick review.

1. Laodicea's water came from two other cities.

2. One aqueduct brought it mineral rich hot water and the other brought in fresher mountain run-off.

3. By the time it reached the city, both sources were lukewarm and tasted terrible.

Hot is good, like a nice hot bath or shower, a bowl of hot chicken soup, or a strong hot cup of coffee. Cold is also good, like a nice refreshing glass of ice water on a hot day. Both hot and cold can be considered good and useful. Yet, the "lukewarm" water of Laodicea was of little good.

If we apply this background to the rebuke that Christ gave the church at Laodicea, it is evident He was using the "waters" as an analogy to their own spiritual situation. Instead of being useful for the Lord in furthering his Kingdom, as the hot and cold waters of the area were useful, Jesus compared them to the virtually useless water of their own city. The Lord Jesus was about to rebuke them by "spitting them out of His mouth."

In our popular evangelical culture today, hot usually conveys a spiritual fervor for something. I have heard people say that they are "on fire for Jesus." Cold can be construed on the other hand as being spiritually dead. For example we say that the "church we visited on Sunday was dead—really cold."

While I can see how easy it would be to read these contemporary connotations into the text, I don't believe this is what is being presented here. To the Laodicean church, the hot and cold would have had a positive reference where the lukewarm would not. Jesus rebuke was directed at the lukewarmness of the church.

Jesus isn't saying he honors "coldness." I can't see Jesus telling the believers in the church to reject him. It doesn't make sense.

His rebuke is clearly for disciplining them and not punishing them. How can I say this? Jesus makes it perfectly clear in verse 19, "*Those whom I love, I reprove and discipline, so be zealous and repent.*" There is a difference between being disciplined and punished.

I disciplined my children because I loved them. The purpose of punishment is to inflict a penalty for an offense, which usually will result in fear and guilt. Discipline on the other hand is to train for correction and maturity. Instead of fear and guilt, the outcome of discipline should be security.

I believe that God is not going to punish the believers in Laodicea but discipline them.

God will discipline His children; he doesn't punish them. For example, look at Hebrews 12:5-7: 5 "*My son, do not regard lightly the discipline of the Lord, nor be weary when reproved by him. 6 For the Lord disciplines the one he loves, and chastises every son whom he receives. 7 It is for discipline that you have to endure. God is treating you as sons. For what son is there whom his father does not discipline?"*

God will not tolerate sin and apathy in the lives of his children. History doesn't tell us how God disciplined the Laodicean Church. All we know is what we can read and it was obvious that He was not happy at all with the behavior of His church.

This passage should serve to both motivate and comfort us. It should motivate us in the fact that we have a Lord who will not tolerate sin and spiritual apathy in the lives of His children. This should also give us comfort in that Jesus will not allow sin to go unchecked in our lives— He is working to conform us into His glorious image.

The writer of Hebrews goes on to explain this in verse 11 of chapter 12. *"For the moment all discipline seems painful rather than pleasant, but later it yields the peaceful fruit of righteousness to those who have been trained by it."*

My hope is that this all makes sense to you before we move on into the rest of this chapter.

And so Jesus says, *". . . because you are lukewarm, and neither hot nor cold, I will spit you out of my mouth."*

When John writes this in his letter, they knew exactly what Jesus is saying to them. They knew their city they had bad water. The mineral content was so high that if they drank the water, it would make them sick. I can relate to this somewhat. I lived in Portland Oregon for many years. You can go to the tap in your kitchen and pour yourself a glass of water. It is usually cold and refreshing. When we moved back to Arizona it was a warm October day. We were busy unloading the U-Haul. Forgetting where I was, I went into the house and poured myself a glass of water from the tap. I immediately spit it out of my mouth. It was warm and tasted like chlorine. The metropolitan Phoenix area, literally, has the worst water. Just to give you an idea how bad the drinking water is—in a survey regarding the cleanliness of the tap water in 100 cities, Phoenix came in dead last.

Compared to Phoenix, maybe Laodicean water wasn't so bad.

Enough about Arizona water. So what is the spiritual significance of this?

The church in Laodicea was so spiritually sick that it made our Lord Jesus hurl. Get the picture? Jesus violently vomits out this church because it is so nauseating to him.

The Greek word here is "*emesai*," which means "to vomit." There is another word, "*ptuo*" that means "to spit" that John could have used if that is what he meant. Our English word "emetic" comes from this word. An emetic is a mixture that doctors give a person when they swallow poison; syrup of ipecac is the most well-known. Castor oil is another.

A lukewarm church makes Jesus vomit. Now honestly, it is hard for me to visualize Jesus bending over vomiting. Although I am sure He did at one time or another in his human life. The people in Laodicea knew exactly what Jesus was talking about. It was not a pretty word picture.

Sadly, this church definitely resembles many of the churches in the United States today. John Stott once wrote, "*The Laodicean church was a half-hearted church. Perhaps none of the seven letters is more appropriate to the twentieth century church than this. It describes vividly the respectable, sentimental, nominal, skin-deep religiosity, which is so wide spread among us today. Our Christianity is flabby and anemic, we appear to have taken a lukewarm bath.*"[69]

The Laodicean church is said to be "lukewarm." Being lukewarm refers to Christians who are indifferent or apathetic because they are self-sufficient and self-satisfied. What are some possible characteristics of a lukewarm Christian?

- They are "Christians" who trust more in themselves and their wealth.

- Lukewarm Christians don't want to be saved from their sin; they only want to be saved from the penalty of their sin.

- They don't really hate sin and most of the time they are not truly sorry for it.

- Lukewarm Christians enjoy the "old life" better than the new one Jesus offers.

- Lukewarm Christians will give to charity and to the church as long as it doesn't take away from their standard of living.

- Lukewarm Christians like "playing it safe" by attending church and trying to be somewhat good.

I think that pretty much nails it. The point is God doesn't call us to be comfortable, apathetic and mediocre in our faith and walk. He calls us to trust Him so completely that we are unafraid to put ourselves in situations where we will be in trouble if He doesn't come through.

Lukewarm living and claiming Christ's name simultaneously is utterly disgusting to God. Therefore he violently "vomits them out of his mouth."

Not only was the Laodicean church lukewarm but they had other issues as well. Look at verse 17.

"For you say, I am rich, I have prospered, and I need nothing, not realizing that you are wretched, pitiable, poor, blind, and naked."

What a sad condition! There is a big difference between "you say," and "you are." Our Lord points this difference out. We can say all kinds of things about ourselves. But the Lord knows us and since He is the faithful and true witness, He will tell it like it is.

This church at Laodicea thought they were "God's gift to ministry." They were a self-sufficient church. They were complacent. They had plenty of money. Perhaps they met in nice homes, had gifted teachers, a great choir, a great organ, a great youth ministry and the respect of the community. They thought they were doing well. But when Jesus looks at it, he says, *"You are wretched, pitiful, poor, blind and naked."* Why such a difference in these two views? It is because they were being measured by two different standards. Laodicea was using the standards of the world. It was pleasant, comfortable church, approved by the community around. But Jesus is using the standard of what he intended his church to be like.

The church at Laodicea was made up of Christians who were trusting in themselves and their wealth or what they thought their wealth could buy them. They were rich and prosperous and had no need. They thought they had an over-abundance of material blessings, but by this statement, it shows they were proud and trusting in that richness as though wealth had the power to give them security and happiness. They were in complete denial about their spiritual condition because they made a fundamental mistake of equating material success with spiritual success.

Jesus says to them you may be rich and have wealth according to the world's standards, but in my eyes you are poor. Your pockets may be full, but your hearts are empty.

Jesus says, "*Though you are physically clothed, I see you as spiritually naked.*"

It reminds me of the LORD's words to Samuel: "*. . . Do not look on his appearance or on the height of his stature, because I have rejected him. For the LORD sees not as man sees: man looks on the outward appearance, but the LORD looks on the heart.*" 1 Samuel 16:7

You can look wealthy, spiritual, powerful, successful and educated, and yet be and poor, blind, naked, spiritually impoverished and lukewarm toward the things of God.

He goes on as well to say that they are blind. Again, this would have been quite shocking because one of the things that this city was known for was an ancient eye salve. People would come from miles away in an effort to be cured of their physical blindness. Isn't it ironic that in an area where there is medicine for healing for visual blindness, there is still spiritual blindness. The word here for blind means "opaque." It does not mean blind as in blind as a bat.

When there would be a solar eclipse, my dad would take a piece of glass and with a candle he would smoke the glass, making it opaque. Why? That way we could see the solar eclipse without hurting our eyes. That is the idea here. The idea is that you can't really see clearly because your eyes are clouded over. Again, I think the Lord was talking to them in terms that they could understand in a very personal way.

It is so easy to point the finger at them and yet forget we are in the same boat. We live in affluence and have a lifestyle that is really unparalleled in the history of the world.

Notice in verse 18 what Jesus tells them to do. Notice that it is not a command: "You will do this or else!" Jesus is advising them—counseling them--"OK, this is what I want you to do."

"I counsel you to buy from me gold refined by fire so that you may be rich, and white garments so that you may clothe yourself and the shame of your nakedness may not be seen, and salve to anoint your eyes, so that you may see."

I think the key to this verse are those three little words *"buy from me."* We don't really need anything else but what Jesus offers. What are we to use to buy these things? Just our lives. Jesus wants us to give our lives completely over to Him. We have been bought and paid for by His shed blood. We need to surrender our lives to Him. When we do that He promises us three things:

First, *"gold refined in the fire."* Peter basically helps us to understand this phrase in 1 Peter 1:7. He tells us that our faith is like gold refined in the fire: *". . . so that the tested genuineness of your faith—more precious than gold that perishes though it is tested by fire—may be found to result in praise and glory and honor at the revelation of Jesus Christ."* Our faith is refined through the testing and trials in our lives. It is similar to the processes used to refine precious and raw metals like steel.

My grandfather was a supervisor for U. S. Steel in Pittsburgh during its steel-making heyday. He was in charge of the open-hearth furnaces. I used to love to listen to him and his buddies sitting around talking about making steel. It didn't sound too different from women talking about what went into baking a cake. He used to tell me about the guys who raked the steel. Just before the molten steel would be tapped and poured into casts or rolled into sheets, men would use long rakes to pull off all the slag and impurities that had risen to the top. In the same way, this refining in our lives tests the genuineness of our faith.

Our faith in what?

Our faith in God and our faith in His Word. Christians cannot function without faith. I have learned that I certainly can't. We were created to live by faith. We say we have faith in God but do we really? Do we trust Jesus daily for everything in our lives? I would guess that most Christians really don't. Why should we? Like the Laodiceans we are self-made.

Look at what fills our lives. Jobs, a house, cars, retirement accounts, health insurance, life insurance, sports, gyms, and vacations. We have every type of electronic convenience to make our lives livable. Even the churches we attend have all the bells and whistles. What more do we need? Do you really need God in your life?

Secondly, Jesus says to buy from him "*white garments so that they may clothe themselves.*"

Everyone is morally naked before God. Every one of us have done things in our lives that we would not want anyone else to know. But God knows! He sees us in our nakedness. What does he offer for it? The righteousness of Christ! All through these letters we have seen that white clothes stand for redemption, for righteousness imparted by Christ. All of our religious or moral good works, if done without Christ, are but filthy rags (Isa. 64:6).

We are no longer to be clothed with our own self-righteousness, but we are to be clothed with the righteousness of Christ himself, a perfect righteousness which God accepts.

Thirdly, Jesus tells them to buy *"salve to anoint your eyes, so that you may see."* Though Laodicea was noted for their eye ointment, Jesus says they need spiritual eye salve that will enable them to see.

I believe this most likely refers to the person and work of the Holy Spirit who anoints our eyes to discern His Word. (John 14:26; 1 Cor. 2:14-16)

The Laodiceans would be enlightened to see what was really spiritual and what wasn't. To see what life is truly about and quit playing religious games. We need to learn to focus on the internals instead of focusing on the externals.

Verse 19: "*Those whom I love, I reprove and discipline, so be zealous and repent.*"

We need to remember that these letters were (and still are) written for the church, for believers in Christ. There might have been unbelievers in their midst, they really were not a part of the church. Christ is addressing believers here and says, "*those whom I love, I reprove and discipline.*"

He loves them and promises to reprove and discipline them to bring them out of their self-sufficiency and into the sufficiency of His life.

This could require severe testing, pain and heartache to bring them (or any believer in this state) to a point of personal need and dependency upon the Lord (Hebrews 12:5-15).

I learned this the hard way after my first wife Jannise died. I was angry, hurt, and disappointed. I am ashamed to say that I didn't handle her death well at all. For over a year I walked away from God and did things I am not proud of. I call this time my "Nebuchadnezzar years." If you are wondering what I am talking about you can read about it in Daniel 4:28-37. During that time I turned my back on

God and went my own way. But just as Nebuchadnezzar's sanity returned, so did mine. But in the process, I also paid dearly for my sins. I learned a hard lesson during that time, God is not to be mocked. There was severe testing, pain and heartache before I finally turned my eyes back towards the Lord. I repented of my sins and was restored.

Likewise, Jesus is warning them to become zealous and to repent of their ways. In other words, repent in order to stop the discipline before it begins. A lesson I'm sure many of us learn the hard way.

The word for *zealous* is in the present imperative, which commands a continual state. We are to continuously maintain our zealousness for Christ. What does zealous mean? It means to be passionate, enthusiastic, committed, and, at times, even fanatical. How are we to do this? We are to maintain this zealous attitude via the means God has given us, through His Word, prayer, the filling of the Holy Spirit and fellowship with other believers, etc.

The word repent is in the aorist imperative, which means do it now. Don't wait, do it right now. Repent means to "to change the mind." Jesus wants the Laodiceans to repent now!

It seems to me that Jesus is obviously frustrated with this church. What more can He say? What more can He do? They just don't get it. It could even be that they didn't want to get it.

So what does He do? He could have just walked away and let judgment fall. But He chooses to wait patiently. And He concludes with these well-known words: *"Behold, I stand at the door and knock. If anyone hears my voice and opens the door, I will come in to him and eat with him, and he with me."*

This passage is more often used in presenting the Gospel and in offering salvation to a lost sinner. Nice thought, but it is incorrect in the context. Jesus is talking to His church. Followers of Jesus Christ. Not unbelievers.

Let's break down this verse. "Behold," that is a polite way of saying "Hey—listen up—pay attention." Jesus literally has been and will continue to stand at the door. The question is what door? Many people say it is the door to your heart. I believe that is incorrect. Think about it. This being the door to your heart is (1) total unbiblical and (2) totally foreign and out of context for this passage. Would it not seem more appropriate to understand this as the door in context to the Laodicean church?

The church was saying it was rich and was in need of nothing, especially Jesus. So no wonder he is depicted as standing outside the door knocking which is in the present tense which means He is continually knocking.

You are probably all familiar with the famous painting "Christ at Heart's Door" by Warner Sallman. If you are not, you could Google it (Sorry, I couldn't get the rights to use it in my book). I have loved looking at this painting since I was a small kid. This painting and its title is probably one of the reasons people have believed that Jesus is knocking on the door to our hearts. If you look at the painting, you can see that there is no latch or knob on the door, meaning that you have to let Jesus in if you want Him to enter.

Although this passage doesn't say there is or isn't a handle or latch, I think there is some truth to this. In my opinion, we have excluded Christ from our churches I believe He is still patiently waiting there for us to open the door.

Jesus goes on to say, "*If anyone who hears My voice, and opens the door, I will come in to him.*"

Basically each of us is given a choice; when we hear the Lord's voice, we can either open the door or not open the door.

I am going to camp hear for a minute and explain some Greek grammar. It is important that you understand these words. It may seem petty but it is quite important.

The phrase "come in" in the Greek is one word *eiseleusomai*. It is followed by the preposition *pros* which in

English means "to." If the writer intended to say come into someone's heart with the idea on entering into it, the word would be expressed with the Greek independent preposition *eis*. However, the Greek preposition *pros* means, "toward," not into.

In all eight instances in the usage of *eiseleusomai pros* in the New Testament, the meaning is "come in toward" someone (i.e., enter a building, house, etc., so as to be in the presence of someone). It is never a penetration into the person himself/herself.

So what is this verse saying? That Jesus Christ will come into the assembly of the Laodicean Church, not into a person. When He comes into the church, He will eat dinner with them. That is, He will have fellowship with them. This Greek word, *deipnēsō*, was used not only of the chief meal of the day but of the meal, which was the occasion for hospitality and fellowship. The picture Jesus is using here of eating an evening meal together speaks of intimate fellowship between the closest of friends. This intimate fellowship is toward the

Christian community as a whole. Since the church or assembly is made up of individual people, this invitation is a call to every member to respond, that the promise of renewal might come to the whole church.

As you can see, this is not a call to an individual to open their heart up to invite Jesus in. This is a promise of mutual companionship with Jesus Christ. Again, this is not an offer of salvation. Rather, it is a promise of Christ's fellowship for any lukewarm believer who repents. If I am wrong, I'll buy the first round in heaven!

Not only does Jesus promise to come into the life of the one who invites Him, but also He promises another special blessing to those who overcome. He has promised the privilege of sitting with Him on His throne. This means the privilege and right to share in Christ's authority and rule in the millennium and eternal future.

Look at verse 21. *"The one who conquers, I will grant him to sit with me on my throne, as I also conquered and sat down with my Father on his throne."*

You may be asking yourself, *"Isn't it going to get a little crowded with all of us up in His lap at the same time?"* Of course that is not what Jesus means. As Jesus rules from His throne, we will rule alongside Him. Again, as we have seen in the last three letters, the promise is to share in our Lord's reign. The true church (those who conquer) are intended to reign with Christ. But our Lord makes a very clear distinction here. Notice how he distinguishes between His throne and His Father's throne.

The Father's throne, of course, is God the Father who governs the universe. The whole universe is under His control. That is the

Father's throne. But Jesus too has a throne. He calls it "my throne." The conquering Christian is invited to reign with him. In Scripture that throne is called the "Throne of David."

When the angel Gabriel appeared to Mary, as recorded in the first chapter of Luke, he told her that she would have a son, and that he would be called the Son of God, and that the Lord God would give to him "the throne of his father David, and he would reign over the house of Jacob forever," Luke 1:32-33.

The house of Jacob is the nation of Israel; all twelve tribes are descended from the sons of Jacob. So this particular promise is relating to the time yet to come when Jesus assumes the throne of David and Israel is made the head of the nations. Of course, we are talking about the millennial kingdom, which has been mentioned several times in these letters already. The church, already being resurrected and glorified, is to share with Him in that reign. I can't fit that into my brain. Someday we will co-rule the nations with Jesus as our head.

And you thought we were just going to sit around playing harps in heaven. Not even close.

I find this absolutely unbelievable. What a great promise. When God says He will exalt you, that's exactly what He means.

And then in verse 22, He closes as He always does. *"He who has an ear, let him hear what the Spirit says to the churches."*

Amen!

Questions for Thoughtful Discussion

1. Are you a new creation in Christ? What are some of the ways that God has changed your life? If you have not experienced any true changes, what does that tell you about your spiritual life?

2. How would you describe your spiritual condition right now? Hot/ Cold/ Lukewarm? If you consider yourself lukewarm towards the things of God, how would you go about changing your spiritual condition?

3. Take some time and think about this next question. Answer as honestly as you can. Do you really need the Holy Spirit to live your life? What percentage of the day would you say you are aware of His presence? Would you say that the life you live now quenches the Spirit of God?

4. The Bible teaches us that the Holy Spirit *teaches* us (John 16:12-13) Do you allow the Spirit to teach you? The Bible says that the Holy Spirit *leads* us (Romans 8:13-14). Do you follow the Holy Spirit's leading? The Bible says that the Holy Spirit *speaks to us* (John 16:13; Acts 10:19; Acts 8:26-29; Acts 13:2) Do you

hear the Spirit's voice when He speaks? The Bible says that the Holy Spirit gives **gifts** (1 Corinthians 12:1,7,11) Do you know your spiritual gift? If so are you using it? The Bible says that the Holy Spirit **causes us to pray and be thankful** (Ephesians 5:18-21). Are you supernaturally thankful? Do you have a meaningful prayer life? Just a few things to work on in your spare time.

5. On a scale of 1-10, with 1 being "Jesus who?" and 10 representing being totally sold out for Jesus, how zealous are you for the Lord?

6. Is Jesus still knocking at the door of your life, asking you to allow Him to become a part of your life? Regardless of where you are spiritually, He wants to have a relationship with you.

Chapter 9

FINAL THOUGHTS —
"Where do you go from here?"

So where do we go from here?

We have defined the church.

We have looked at Jesus letters to the seven churches.

Can we learn anything from these seven churches?

I guess a better question would be *"what have you learned from the study of these seven churches?"* Jesus reminds us at the end of each message to the churches: *"Anyone with ears to hear must listen to the Spirit and understand what he is saying to the churches."*

So . . . have you heard from the Spirit of God?

Do you understand what it means to be filled and empowered by the Spirit of God?

Do you hear and recognize the Spirit's voice in your life?

Do you understand what the Spirit is saying to the Church?"

I have given you a little history of each of the churches. I have shared with you from my heart what I have learned from these passages.

Now the rest is up to you. I don't have a clue to what the Spirit of God has for your life. I do know that He does have a plan for each of us. And the only way to know the plan God intends for us is to be connected to His Spirit. If you are not daily confessing sin, and walking in the Spirit, you will not know what God's plan is for your life. It is as simple as that. I think a lot of Christians are like that metal ball in a pinball machine. You just bounce thru life with no real direction. Sometimes you hit the right bumper or target, but most of the time you just bounce around until you fall through the out hole. How can you claim to be a Christian and not be connected to the Spirit of God?

Along the same line, do you know what God's will is for your life? God's will is no secret. Do you really think that a loving God would say to His children, "*I have a perfect will for your life. I have hidden it and now it is your job to find it?*"

God doesn't do that. If you want to know God's will for your life, read and memorize Romans 12:1-2. Let's take a quick look at it. "*1 And so, dear brothers and sisters, I plead with you to give your bodies to God because of all he has done for you. Let them be a living and holy sacrifice—the kind He will find acceptable. This is truly the way to worship him. 2 Don't copy the behavior and customs of this world, but let God transform you into a new person by changing the way you think.* **Then you will learn to know God's will for you,** *which is good and pleasing and perfect."*

Did you catch that?

How does God transform our bodies and our minds? He transforms us through the power of His Holy Spirit. As we give our bodies and our thoughts over to the power of the Holy Spirit, it is only then that we can be obedient and follow Him.

Remember what we learned about the church—the *ekklesia*? It is a gathering together of the true follower's of Jesus Christ. If we want to change the world it starts with us. It starts with you and with me.

We are the Church.

We need to be true followers of Jesus Christ.

What do I mean by a true follower of Jesus Christ? In western society the term "Christian" has become very loose. For many people being a Christian seems to simply mean that they might have prayed a prayer for salvation at one time or the other. They might even go to church on Sunday and sing worship songs, occasionally pray, or just simply they believe in God.

Being a true follower of Christ means to change our entire lifestyle. It means to change the way we act, think and speak. In order to be a follower of Jesus we need to change our entire life, dying to who we used to be and becoming a new people (2 Corinthians 5:17). This takes commitment and sacrifice and it is not easy. I know this for a fact because I still struggle with it everyday.

Do I allow the Spirit of God to control my life or do ignore Him? We allow our lives to take precedence over our walk with God. The "things of this earth" take over priority in our lives. Oh, we may want to change, but it is just takes too much effort and time.

And so we give up.

As church leaders, too often we have undersold the Gospel. We have tried to make it easy in order to convince others to accept it, but again there is a cost to following Jesus. The plain truth is that we don't want to give up what we have materially in this world. More importantly, we don't want to turn our lives totally over to God. We like being in control. If we can somehow fit Jesus into an hour or so during our busy week we are doing good. He will understand, right?

We need to be totally sold out to Him. He needs to be first place in our lives—period—no excuses. We will never impact this world, our communities or even our families if we are living a superficial faith.

I guess the honest question is this: Are you willing to fully give your life over to Jesus Christ no matter the cost? Do you know what that means? Are you willing to count the cost?

One of the things about Christianity is that it was never intended to be merely an intellectual exercise. Following Jesus Christ goes far beyond believing certain things about God. It gets down to the issue of obedience, commitment, and change.

Imagine Peter saying to Jesus: *"Lord, I would love to come with you. But couldn't we just do everything in a way that won't interfere with the plans I already have in place? I've got plans for my life."*

That would have been a natural response. And, for many years, that was my response to God. *"Thanks for saving me . . . I'll probably see you in church on Sunday . . . but I've got things to do and places to see."* I had never really turned my "whole" life over to God.

By God's grace, the disciples gave up everything they had to follow Him. Are our lives more important or any different than theirs?

Are you willing to have your life changed to reflect God's agenda, or do you expect God to fit into your agenda?

I would say that the reason the church in America is in such poor condition is the lack of discipleship. I already mentioned that in the introduction. I am not talking about programs—heaven only knows we have programs coming out of our ears. One of the symptoms of the lack of discipleship in the church is that we do not know *what* we believe and, secondly, *who* we are in Christ. As Christian syndicated columnist Cal Thomas says about lack of discipleship: *"The problem in our culture . . . isn't the abortionists. It isn't the pornographers or drug dealers or criminals. It is the undisciplined, undiscipled, disobedient and biblically ignorant Church of Jesus Christ."* [69]

I couldn't have said it any better.

The lack of discipleship in the church today results in shallow commitment, apathy, biblical ignorance and the inability to do advanced Christian ministry. I have talked with many pastors and church leaders over the years. When I ask them if they have discipleship groups going in their churches, the answer is usually a resounding *yes!* At that point I ask a few more specific questions and it becomes clearly evident that there is really no true discipling going on in their churches. Just because they have a Saturday morning men's ministry that regularly prays over a bowl of Fruit Loops doesn't make it a discipleship group. True discipleship is men and women pouring their lives into other people. Walking side-by-side through life for at least a year—maybe more. That is why most people don't do discipleship. It is just plain to hard and takes up a lot of time and energy.

It is not flashy! But the rewards are eternally rewarding.

One of the illustrations I use when I disciple someone is the "Parable of the Two Wells."[70] My life was drastically changed years ago when someone shared with me this illustration. This illustration will answer both issues I mentioned earlier:

1) Not knowing who we are in Christ and—
2) How to walk in the power of the Holy Spirit.

If you can put to practice daily the principles in this illustration, I can guarantee your life will change.

I first saw this illustration in the book "***Personal Disciplemaking: A Step-By-Step Guide for Leading a New Christian from New Birth to Maturity***" by Chris Adsit. It is the best how-to book on discipleship out there. I highly recommend it because I still use it today.

The Parable of the Two Wells

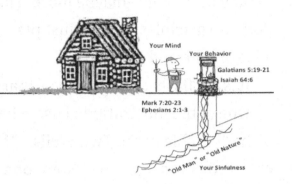

The way you were before you became a Christian could be represented by this well. The farmer who owned this well used it all the time. It was the farmer's only source of water. The trouble was that the water that came out this well was contaminated. The underground stream that fed the well ran under a toxic waste dump so the farmer and his family always felt weak and ill. But since they had drunk from that well all their lives, they didn't know they were sick. This represents the natural or carnal (unsaved) man. This is who you and I were before we met Christ. The farmer represents your *mind*. The underground stream represents your *old self* or your *old nature*. The contamination represents your *sinfulness*. Jesus said in Mark 7:20-23: *". . . It is what comes from inside that defiles you.*

21 For from within, out of a person's heart, come evil thoughts, sexual immorality, theft, murder, 22 adultery, greed, wickedness, deceit, lustful desires, envy, slander, pride, and foolishness. 23 All these vile things come from within; they are what defile you."

Paul said in Ephesians 2:1-3 that we were all like this at one time. It was our nature to be that way. It was who we were. But just as the farmer and his family had only one well to go to, and they weren't aware of the contamination, likewise we had only one character to draw on, and it too was contaminated (sinful and depraved). And so just as the farmer and his family were headed to an early grave, we were headed for an eternal grave. Paul tells us about the kinds of behavior that this contaminated well produces in Galatians 5:19-21 (The works of the flesh): 19 *"When you follow the desires of your sinful nature, the results are very clear: sexual immorality, impurity, lustful pleasures, 20 idolatry, sorcery, hostility, quarreling, jealousy, outbursts of anger, selfish ambition, dissension, division, 21 envy, drunkenness, wild parties, and other sins like these. Let me tell you again, as I have before, that anyone living that sort of life will not inherit the Kingdom of God."*

Isaiah tells us in Isaiah 64:6 that the best we can be in this condition are like "filthy rags" to God.

One day a man from the Environmental Protection Agency (EPA) came and tested the farmer's well. He alerted the farmer to the contamination. Immediately the farmer stopped using his well, but he still needed water. So he consulted with some well-drilling experts and they informed him that there was a crystal clear underground stream on the other side of the property. He sent down another well shaft and sure enough, the water he found there was perfectly pure.

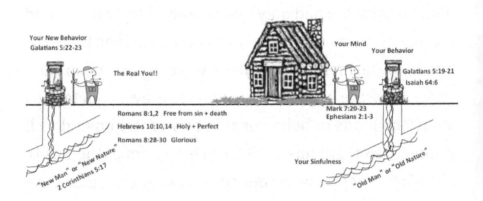

This is who you are when you decided to become a follower of Christ. This underground stream represents the "new you." You now have a new nature. The good news is it has no contaminating sin nature.

2 Corinthians 5:17 tells us: "*. . . anyone who belongs to Christ has become a new person. The old life is gone; a new life has begun!*"

God has made you a whole new creation with a whole new character and nature. Galatians 5:22-23 talks about the kind of behavior that will come out of this "pure well."

22 *"But the Holy Spirit produces this kind of fruit in our lives: love, joy, peace, patience, kindness, goodness, faithfulness, 23 gentleness, and self-control. There is no law against these things!"*

This new man is the opposite from the old man. Romans 8:1-2 talks about how the law of the Spirit of life has set us free from the law of sin and death, just like the pure water of this well set the farmer and his family free from the sickness and death of his contaminated well. The new true new nature of the believer is now one of righteousness, completeness and perfection. Hebrews 10:10, 14 talks about how we have been made (Notice the past tense) holy and perfect. 10 *"For God's will was for us to be made holy by the sacrifice of the body of Jesus Christ, once for all time. 14 "For by that one offering he forever made perfect those who are being made holy.*

Romans 8:28-30 tells us that in God's eyes we are already glorified.

This well represents the new you. It is the real you. All because of what Christ has done.

Now, there is a problem with all of this. Sometimes we are not loving. Sometimes we are not joyful. And if you hadn't noticed—we still sin! How is it, if we have this new nature within us we can still sin? The reason you and I still have the ability, even the inclination to continue

263

sinning is that just as the farmer's contaminated well sits right next to his house, our old nature still exists within us. So, sometimes we decide to go back to the old well and draw from it.

The farmer may, from time-to-time, thinks it's too far to walk to the new well. After all, it is on the other side of the property. The old well is right outside the door. Or maybe he doubted the man from the EPA's test. Or he could rationalize "just a little bit won't hurt."

In the same, way our minds find it easier to draw from our old nature. We may be so used to following the dictates of our old nature that we completely forget about the new nature God has given us. For thirty years, when the farmer wanted water he just walked out the door and turned left. It may take him a while to remember to turn right.

Paul talks about this in Romans 7:18-25. Just as the farmer truly wants to quit drinking the contaminated water so Paul wants to quit following the dictates of his old nature. It is not easy. In fact Paul calls it a "war" (verse 23).

In the end . . . Paul says that the only way he'll be able to do it is with God's help. This is where the ministry of the Holy Spirit comes in. The Spirit is like a big neon sign planted right outside the farmer's front door flashing "Turn Right!"

The farmer can still choose to disregard the sign. In the same way we can choose to disregard the direction of the Holy Spirit. That is why it is ultimately going to be up to each of us to choose which well we draw from. God will help us . . . but the decision is ours to make.

Paul says in Ephesians 4:20-24 that we should "Put off" our old selves and "Put on" our new selves. It requires an act of our will every day.

A few years ago my father-in-law purchased a red convertible 2001 BMW Z8. It had a 32-valve V8 that developed 400 hp. It was a sweet car. I was always too afraid to drive it, but enjoyed being a passenger while my father-in-law drove. One day we were driving on the country roads just outside of Beaverton, Oregon. There wasn't much traffic on this old road so my father-in-law opened it up. It handled those old, winding country roads so well.

After about 20 minutes I noticed one of the "idiot lights" on the dash start to blink orange I said, "Don, what is that flashing light on the dashboard mean?"

"Oh, don't worry about it, it is only the oil light. It always comes on, just ignore it," he said.

So we ignored the light. A few minutes later another light came up on the dashboard. Again I brought his attention to the red light. This time it was the temperature warning light. Again he told me not to worry about it. Before long just about every light on the dash was either blinking or beeping. I again brought his attention to the lights. Don said, "Aren't they pretty . . . just like twinkling Christmas lights."

You have probably figured out by now that this is not a true story. I just made it up. But let me ask you, what would have happened if this was a true story and he ignored all those warning lights on his dash?

It would seriously destroy the engine of his car.

The Holy Spirit in your life can be somewhat like the "idiot lights" that are on your car's dash. The lights are there to warn you that something is going on in your engine. The Holy Spirit is there to warn us about things going on in our lives. Just like the blinking arrows in the

266

illustration about the well, you and I, each moment of our lives, must make a decision to either turn right and obey the Spirit of God or rebel and turn left. There are times in my life when I hear the Spirit's voice and in obedience I follow. And then there are those times when I basically tell the Spirit to "take a hike" and I willfully choose to follow my own path. If I choose to disobey the Spirit over a long period of time, I usually find myself in trouble. It is not too long afterward that I will usually come to my senses and repent and confess my sin and then I am back in the grace of God.

Each day, every moment, we all have a decision to make. Which well do we drink from? If we drink from the wrong well and sin, then we need to repent and confess our sin and return to walking in obedience to the Spirit.

Once, a wise old man, who had walked with the Lord for many years, was talking with his teenage grandson who had recently become a Christian.

"Grandpa, I just can't get the hang of this Christian life. Sometimes I feel close to God and have no trouble obeying Him. Other times I want to do and say all kinds of things that I know are wrong. Why can't I be good all the time?"

"Well, son, let me tell you something I learned a long time ago. Following Jesus is a lot like having two dogs living inside of you. One is a good dog and the other is bad and they are fighting all the time."

"That sure sounds like me. I guess the bad dog wins more than the good dog. Which one wins in you Grandpa?"

The grandpa said, "The one I feed."

Many Christians still obey the demands of their old nature for several reasons. The first is out of habit. We get so stuck in the rut that it is hard climb out. It is too hard to change. The second reason is fear or resignation. They have tried and they just can't change. They are in sin too strongly. Lastly, they stay put out of ignorance. They don't understand who they are in Christ.

So, what do you need to do?

Learn, understand, and live out who you are in Christ Jesus. You need to learn to walk in the Spirit of God and be obedient. Confessing and repenting of sin should be as natural as breathing air. It is hard to do, but you need to allow the Spirit to help you. It will become easier. That is why Paul urges us in Romans 12:1-2 to be transformed by the "renewing of our mind." Our minds have to be re-taught to draw upon the supernatural resources of our new nature instead of the contamination of the old nature.

My prayer is that you will allow the Living God to totally transform your life so that you will become more like His Son Jesus Christ. How do we change the world and the church? One person at a time and it starts with me and you. It will also take a lot of prayer. Are you up for the challenge?

"Do you believe that what you believe is really real? Because if you really believe that what you believe is real, then Christians will change the world."

Quote by Del Tackett, Former President of Focus on the Family, *The Truth Project*, 2008.

Questions for Thoughtful Discussion

1. Do you understand what it means to you to be a "new creation" in Christ?

2. Do you understand why you still have sinful urges, despite being born again?

3. Do you understand that it is your decision whether you decide to follow the dictates of your old self or your new nature?

4. When was the last time you allowed the Spirit of God to have access to your life?

5. How can you keep from acting like your old creation? What are some actions you can take to keep from going back to the "old well?"

6. Find someone who will disciple you and commit to being disciple for at least six months.

Footnotes for Book

Introduction:

1 R.A. Torrey, *How to Obtain Fullness of Power* (Whitaker House: New Kensington, PA, 1982,84) 71.

2 J. C. Ryle, *Holiness: Its Nature, Hindrances, Difficulties, and Roots*, (Hendrickson Publishing: Peabody, MA 2007) 299.

3 Dr. Howard Hendricks, Message, *"Expand or Expire: Spiritual Growth,"* The Discipleship Library, https://www.discipleship library.com

4 Barna, George, and Frank Viola. *Pagan Christianity? – Exploring the Roots of Our Church Practices*, (Carol Stream, IL: Tyndale HP, 2008), xxxi.

5 George R. Hunsberger and Craig Van Gelder, editors, *The Church Between the Gospels and Culture*, (Grand Rapids, MI: Eerdmans, 1996), 149.

6 Barna, George, and Frank Viola. *Pagan Christianity? – Exploring the Roots of Our Church Practices*, (Carol Stream, IL: Tyndale HP, 2008), 107.

7 AD Nock, *Conversion*, (Oxford: Clarendon Press, 1933), 212.

8 Henry Bettenson and Chris Maunder, editors, *Documents of the Christian Church, 3rd. ed.*, (Oxford UP, 1999), 2.

9 Frank Viola, George Barna, *Pagan Christianity? Exploring the Roots of Our Church Practices*, 193. In the early first and second centuries, the Lord's Supper seems to have been taken in the evening as a meal. Second century sources show it was taken only on Sundays. In the Didache, the Eucharist is still shown to be taken with the Agape meal (love feast).

Chapter 1 What is the Church?

10 *The Pew Forum on Religion and Public Life*, December 19, 2011 (Gordon-Conwell Theological Seminary: South Hamilton, MA)

11 Joseph Thayer, *Greek-English Lexicon of the New Testament*, (Grand Rapids, MI: Baker, 1977), 196

12 Flavius Josephus (Author), William Whiston (Translator), *The Works of Josephus: The Learned and Authentic Jewish Historian, and Celebrated Warrior*, (Philadelphia, PA: Published by J. Grigg, 1829).

13 Clement of Alexandria, *The Instructor*, Book 3, chapter 11.

14 Graydon F. Snyder, *Ante Pacem: Archaeological Evidence of Church Life Before Constantine*, (Macon, GA: Mercer University Press, 1985), 67.

15 Graydon F. Snyder, *First Corinthians: A Faith Community Commentary*, (Macon, GA: Mercer University Press, 1991), 3.

16 Michael Frost, *On Being the Missional Church*, Presbyterian Global Fellowship Conference (Houston, TX) 2007

17 *The Apology of Aristides the Philosopher*, around 125 AD from Section XV

18 Ramsey McMullen, Eugene N. Lane editors, *Paganism and Christianity*, 100-425 C.E. A Sourcebook (Fortress Press: Minneapolis, MN 1992) pp. 271-272

Chapter 2 Ephesus

19 Burt Bacharach and Hal David, "*What the World Needs Now Is Love Sweet Love*," Copyright 1965 BLUE SEAS MUSIC, INC. & JAC MUSIC CO., INC. International Copyright Secured

20 "*They Will Know We Are Christians By Our Love*," Copyright 1966 Peter Scholtes, F.E.I. (Licensed)

21 David Kinnamen, Gabe Lyons, "*Un-christian: What A New Generation Really Thinks About Christianity*," Editorial; *Christianity Today*, 2007

22 Robert L. Thomas Kenneth, *The Cayster River, Turkey's Cayster River, Then and Today, An Exegetical Commentary*, Revelation 1-7, copyright 2013 (Moody Press: Chicago 1992) pp.128-130

23 Edwin Yamauchi, *New Testament Cities In Western Asia Minor: Light From Archeology On Cities of Paul and the*

Seven Churches, (Nipf and Stock Publishers: Eugene, OR 2003) p. 103

24 J.T. Marlin, *The Seven Churches of Asia Minor*, (J.T. Marlin Publisher: Harrisburg, VA 1980) 36

25 *Brewer's Dictionary of Phrase and Fable*, (Philadelphia: Henry Altemus Company 1898) 1440

26 John MacArthur, *Ephesians, MacArthur New Testament Commentary*, (Moody Bible Institute of Chicago, 1986) p.166

27 Joshua J. Mark, *Ephesos, Ancient History Encyclopedia*, published 9/2/2009

28 Kimberley Christine Patton, *Religion of the Gods: Ritual, Paradox, and Reflexivity: Ritual, Paradox*, (Published Oxford University Press: New York, NY, 2009), p. 118

29 Tertullian, *Apologeticum*, (The Apology), Chapter 40

30 Benny Hinn, audio clip recorded Dec. 31, 1989, at Orlando Christian Center.

31 Cyril, C. Richardson, *The Library of Christian Classics: Early Church Fathers, Volume 1*, (Philadelphia: The Westminster Press, 1953) Pg. 9

32 Words and music by Barry Man, Cynthia Weil and Phil Spector, *"You've Lost That Lovin' Feeling,"* 1964-65 Screen Gems-EMI Music, and Mother Bertha Music, Inc., Philles Records

33 Statistics provided by The Fuller Institute, George Barna, and Pastoral Care Inc. Copyright © 2014 Pastoral Care Inc.

Chapter 3 Smyrna

34 Tom Heneghan, Religion Editor, *"About 100 million Christians persecuted around the world: report,"* Reuters.com, 2013

35 (From The New Unger's Bible Dictionary. Originally published by Moody Press of Chicago, Illinois. Copyright (c) 1988.)

36 *Statue of a Drunken Old Woman.* Vinum Nostrum. Museo Galileo, n.d. Web. 1 Dec. 2012.

37 *Izmir*, http://www.turizm.net/cities/izmir/ Turizm,net 2010

38 Preaching Today Citation: George F. MacLeod, Leadership, Volume 2, no. 4.

39 Marvin Phillips, *Never Lick A Frozen Flagpole*, (Howard Publishing Co. West Monroe, LA 1999) 64

Chapter 4 Pergamum

40 Michael Horton, *"Beyond Culture Wars,"* *Modern Reformation* (May-June 1993), p. 3

41 Tim Stafford, *"The Third Coming of George Barna,"* *Christianity Today*, August 8, 2002, p. 34.

42 George Barna, *Think Like Jesus*, (Integrity, 2003), p. 40.

43 Gallup and Roper Organization survey results in National and International Religion Reports (October 1990), 8.

44 Dan Edelen, Cerulean Sanctus: *Why Christianity is Failing in America*, November 13, 2009

45 George Barna, *Futurecast: What Today's Trends Mean for Tomorrow's World*, (Tyndale Publishing House: Carol Stream, IL 2012) 268.

46 John S. Dickerson, *The Great Evangelical Recession: 6 Factors That Will Crash the American Church . . . and How to Prepare*, (Baker Publishing Group: Grand Rapids, MI 2013) p33

47 Robert H. Mounce, *The Book of Revelation, The New International Commentary on the New Testament*," [Grand Rapids: Eerdmans, 1977], 95

48 Kekeç 1989, p. 40

49 Bible Study in Paradise Valley, Josh McDowell talked on dangers of pornography, 2014

50 Rachel Sussman, LCSW, *2014 "State of Dating In America Survey*," ChristianMingle.com, JDating.com http://cerule-ansanctum.com/

Chapter 5 Thyatira

51 William Lobdell, "*Pollster Prods Christian Conservatives,*" *LA Times*, 2002-SEP-14, at http://www.latimes.com/features/religion/

52 Apologist Josh McDowell: "*Internet the Greatest Threat to Christians,*" *The Christian Post* – US By Anugrah Kumar, Christian Post Contributor, July 2011

53 William Barclay, *Letters to the Seven Churches*, (Westminster John Knox Press: Louisville, KY 2001) pg. 47

54 How would I explain Dispensationalism to a novice? Dispensationalism is basically a biblical interpretation, which states that God has and will use several different means of administering His will to both Jews and Gentiles during different periods of history. I personally believe there are seven chronologically successive periods. We believe in a literal interpretation of scripture with a pre-millennial and pre-tribulation rapture view. It sees Israel and the church as separate distinct bodies. The seven main dispensation are: Innocence (Genesis 1-3) Conscience (Genesis 3-8) Civil Government (Genesis 9-11) Promise (Genesis 12-Ex. 19) Law (Exodus

20-Acts 2:4) Grace (Acts 2:4-Revelation 20:3) Millennial Kingdom (Rev. 20:4-6) (Exodus 20-Acts 2:4) Grace (Acts 2:4-Revelation 20:3) Millennial Kingdom (Rev. 20:4-6)

Chapter 6 Sardis

55 *"Sardis or Sardis Turkey."* The Princeton Encyclopedia of Classical Sites. 1976. Tufts University, Princeton, N.J.

56 The concept of *"cathedral of consumption"* was coined by the distinguished professor and sociologist George Ritzer (1999, 2007).

57 R.A. Tozer, *I Call It Heresy*, (Harrisburg, PA: Christian Publications, 1974) p. 5

58 Gary Langer, *"Poll: Most Americans Say They're Christian,"* ABC News, July 2014, abcnews.go.com

59 Dr. Tony Evans, *The Victorious Christian Life* (Nashville: Nelson, 1994), 249-50

Chapter 7 Philadelphia

60 Keitel, E. (2010). *"Tacitus and the Disaster Narrative"*. In Kraus C.S., Marincola J. & Pelling C. Ancient Historiography and Its Contexts: Studies in Honour of A. J. Woodman. Oxford University Press. p. 335.

61 William Barclay, *"The Revelation of John, Volume I,"* (The Westminster Press, Philadelphia), p. 158.

62 Tom Phillips, *"Liushi, Zhejiang province, China On Course to Become 'World's Most Christian Nation' Within 15 Years,* "*The Telegraph*, Apr 2014

63 Alex Murashko, Christian Post Reporter, *Open Doors: Growth of Christianity in Iran 'Explosive,'* March 23, 2012
www.OpenDoorsUSA.org

Chapter 8 Laodicea

64 A "Big Gulp" is a 44-ounce drink you get at a convenience market in most Western states. Mine was filled usually with Coca Cola or Pepsi.

65 John McRay, *Archaeology And The New Testament*, (Baker Publishing: Grand Rapids, MI, 1991) p. 248

66 David Noel Freedman, Allen C. Myers, Astrid B. Beck, Editors, *Eerdmans Dictionary of the Bible*, (Wm. B. Eerdmans Publishing Company: Grand Rapids, MI, 2000) p. 61

67 William Barclay, *Letters to the Philippians, Colossians and Thessalonians*, p. 93.

68 John R. W. Stott, *"What Christ Thinks of the Church: An Exposition of Revelation 1-3,"* [Baker Book House Company: Grand Rapids, MI

2003) or Escape the Coming Night David Jeremiah Thomas Nelson Publishers 1997, P. 78

Final Thoughts

69 Interview with Cal Thomas, *Christianity Today*, April 25th 1994

70 Christopher B. Adsit, *"Personal Disciple-Making: A Step-by-Step Guide for Leading A Christian from New Birth to Maturity,"*

If you enjoyed this book, had questions or even disagreed with it, I would love to hear from you. If your church or ministry is interested in starting a discipleship ministry and don't know where to start . . . I would love to chat with you.

If you would like more information about 2wenty-8ight:19 Ministries you can contact me

Chris Copeland
10645 North Tatum
Blvd. 200-518
Phoenix, AZ 85028
(602) 448-9035
2wenty8ight19@gmail.com
driphrog11@yahoo.com
Website: www.cmi-ministries-org

CPSIA information can be obtained
at www.ICGtesting.com
Printed in the USA
FSOW03n0738241215
14671FS

9 781498 440363